G000129181

THE GOLDEN SHORE

VERLAGSGESELLSCHAFT GMBH

222
Meditation Techniques

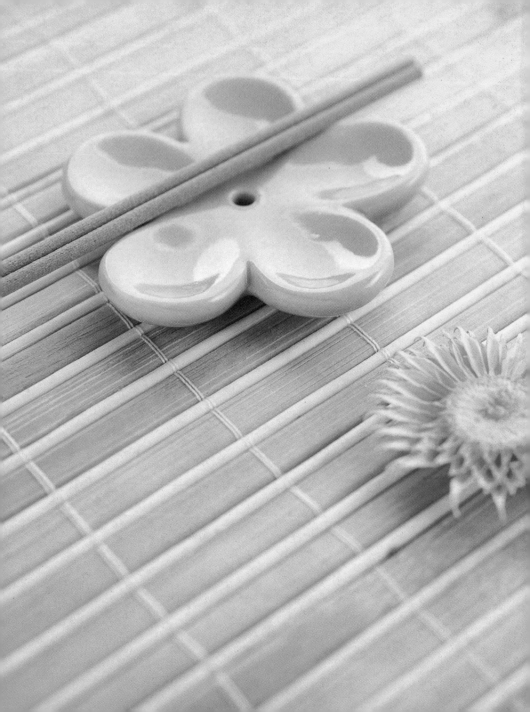

222
Meditation Techniques

from the writings of

SRI CHINMOY

Copyright © 2016 Sri Chinmoy Centre

All rights reserved. No portion of this book may be reproduced in
any form without express written permission from the Publisher.

ISBN 978-3-89532-287-7
Bird drawings are selection from Soul-Bird series by Sri Chinmoy.
Back cover photograph courtesy of Ranjana Ghose.

Published by The Golden Shore Verlags GmbH
Austraße 74, 90429 Nürnberg • Germany
www.bluebeyondbooks.co.uk

Printed in the Czech Republic.

Contents

89 Visualisations . . . .

99 Guided meditations . . . .

Developing good qualities 113

Meditations for runners 163

Meditations for everyday life 173

Preface

Whether meditation is something new to you or an established practice in your life, the discovery of the endless treasures that it brings is an ever-unfolding adventure. Meditation is a path leading us within; we follow it with the help of aspiration—our inner cry for happiness, love and truth. Once we begin to discover the beauty of a silent mind and a peace-flooded heart, we realise that this inner journey never ends. Not only every day but every moment of quietude or meditation will bring us increasing joy and fulfilment. Meditation will enrich our daily life and ultimately lead us to the realisation of our inmost essence—that shining, all-pervading and transcendent reality that we, according to our understanding, call God, the Supreme, Truth or Love. We hope that this collection of meditation techniques from Sri Chinmoy's writings will inspire you on the journey ahead.

—*The Editors*

Introduction

It is only through meditation that we can get lasting peace, divine peace. If we meditate soulfully in the morning and receive peace for only one minute, that one minute of peace will permeate our whole day. And when we have a meditation of the highest order, then we get really abiding peace, light and delight. We need meditation because we want to grow in light and fulfil ourselves in light. If this is our aspiration, if this is our thirst, then meditation is the only way.

In my writings I have described many techniques for meditation. The individual seeker has to choose the way that will help him make the fastest progress. But no matter which technique one uses, aspiration is of paramount importance. The inner aspiration has infinitely more power than outer obstacles. If you utilise your inner strength, then circumstances have to surrender to your aspiration. If you really want to meditate every day, then I wish to tell you that your inner aspiration will give you the power to do it.

Just try to set aside a certain time of day when you will try to be calm and quiet, and feel that these five minutes belong to your inner being and to nobody else. Regularity is of paramount importance. What you need is regular practice at a regular time.

The best way to meditate is to sit cross-legged on a small cushion or rug. The spine and the neck must be kept erect. If it is not possible for you to sit that way, then please try, if you are sitting on a chair, to sit with your entire back straight and erect.

If you feel that you can meditate soulfully only once each day, early in the morning, then that is enough. You have to see your real capacity, sincerity, willingness and joy. If you start by doing the right thing early in the morning, then you will be inspired all day.

—*Sri Chinmoy*

Developing concentration

Every seeker should start with concentration in the spiritual life. Concentration has to pave the way for meditation. When we concentrate, we try to control our thoughts, our emotions.

Concentration means inner vigilance, alertness. There are thieves all around us and within us. Fear, doubt, worry and anxiety are inner thieves that try to steal our inner poise and peace of mind. When we are concentrating, we make it hard for these forces to enter into us.

Concentration
Perfects our mind.

Aspiration
Perfects our heart.

Service
Perfects our life.

The tip of your thumb

When you concentrate, you have to feel that nothing
exists except the thing that you are concentrating
upon. When you concentrate, try to forget the rest
of the world: what is within you, around you, before
you, above you, below you. Concentrate on only one
object. If you want to concentrate on the tip of your
thumb, start with imagination. Imagine that your
only possession is your thumb. There is nothing else
which you can claim as your own. The rest of the
body does not belong to you—only the thumb. If you
want to concentrate on the tip of your nose, feel that
you are the possessor of only your nose; you are not
the possessor of your eyes, your ears, your mouth,
your limbs. If you begin to think of something else,
feel that you are entering into foreign territory. In this
way, you will develop your power of concentration.

You are at liberty to choose any part of your body
to concentrate on, but try to use some part which you
feel as your very own. And do not concentrate on your
arm or your hand or your leg. Take a very small part
of your body—the eye or the nose or a fingertip. The
smaller the better for concentration.

The tiniest thing

When you want to acquire the power of concentration, identify yourself with the tiniest thing possible.

Then only will you become all-powerful. God is all-powerful not because He is vastness itself, but because He is inside the ant as well as the elephant. God is all-powerful because He can be both elephant and ant. He is the infinite and He is the finite. Just because He is finite and infinite at the same time, He is omnipotent.

A flame in your heart

Kindly imagine inside your heart[1] a flame. Right now the flame is tiny and flickering; it is not a powerful flame. But one day it will definitely become most powerful and most illumining. So every day before you pray and meditate, try to imagine inside your heart a flame, a burning flame. And please try to imagine that that flame is illumining your mind. You cannot concentrate according to your satisfaction because the mind is not focused. The mind is constantly thinking of many things. It has become a victim of many uncomely thoughts. The mind does not have proper illumination, so imagine a beautiful flame inside your heart, illumining you. Bring that illumining flame inside your mind. Then you will gradually see a streak of light inside your mind. When your mind starts becoming illumined, it is very, very easy to concentrate for a long time, and also to concentrate more deeply.

The sound of your heartbeat

Some seekers like to concentrate on their heartbeat. If you want to do this, do not be afraid that the heart will stop and that you will die. No, if you want to be a real hero in your spiritual life, you can try to concentrate on your heartbeat. This is the golden opportunity for you to enter into the endless life. Each time you hear the sound of your heartbeat, immediately feel there your infinite, immortal life.

If you want to try to hear the sound of your heartbeat, that will be very good. If you fold your hands on top of your heart[1], you will feel your heartbeat. Then, after you develop the power of concentration, you can meditate on your heartbeat in any part of your body. If your mind is bothering you, you can bring the hammer—the heartbeat—there and strike the mind so that it will be good.

A spiritual Master's photograph

When you want to practise concentration, you should choose something that gives you immediate joy. If you have a Master, your Master's picture will give you immediate joy. If you don't have a Master, select something that is very beautiful, divine and pure, like a flower, for example.

As pure as a flower

For this exercise you will need a flower. Please look at the entire flower for a few seconds, and while you are concentrating on it, try to feel that you yourself are this flower. At the same time, try to feel that this flower is growing inside your heart—in the inmost recesses of your heart[1].

Then try to concentrate gradually on one particular petal of the flower. Feel that this petal which you have selected is the seed-form of your reality-existence. After a few minutes, concentrate on the entire flower again, and feel that it is the Universal Reality. In this way, go back and forth, concentrating first on the petal—the seed-form of your reality—and then on the entire flower—the Universal Reality.

While you are doing this, please do not allow any thought to enter into your mind. Try to make your mind absolutely calm, quiet, and tranquil. Also, kindly keep your eyes half open.

After some time, please close your eyes and try to see the flower on which you have been concentrating inside your heart. Then in the same way that you concentrated on the physical flower in your hand, kindly concentrate on the flower inside your heart, with your eyes closed.

A flower signifies purity. Try to feel that your heart has become as pure as the flower.

Purify the breath

If you would like to develop better concentration, before you start your meditation, repeat the Name of God, 'Supreme'[2], about twenty times as fast as possible. First purify your breath by repeating 'Supreme'. The breath has to be purified; unless and until the breath is purified, the mind will wander and cannot remain one-pointed. If the breath is purified, then the mind will not act like a restless monkey.

Grow into the breath of God

Concentrate on your inner divinity. Always try to feel that you are safe when you are with God, with divinity. Let God and the divine qualities within you act against your human, undivine qualities. When you use the word 'God', please try to feel your real love for God. When you are concentrating, feel that you are really growing into God, into the very breath of God. Then your concentration is bound to do something for you.

Become the witness

First you try to focus your attention on a particular object, then you enter into it, then you go beyond it. Then you come back to yourself and you become the witness, or *Sakshapurusha*. This is real concentration. This is the secret of meditation. If you know it, you can concentrate most effectively.

Pierce the object

Take an idea and try to make this idea into a living being. Then place it on the wall at your eye level. If it is too difficult to use an idea, then take some material object and place it on the wall. Keep your eyes open. It is always better to concentrate with open eyes. Look at the object and start concentrating. Now enter into the object. You have to apply all your attention and pierce through the object to the other side. When you have gone to the other side, from there start concentrating. You are there, your body is here. You start concentrating from the other side and from there look at your own body.

THE BLACK DOT ON THE WALL

If you want to achieve extraordinary concentration,
please try these exercises.

Drilling a hole

Stand right in front of a wall, and put a dot on the
wall right at the level of your *third eye³ [the spiritual
centre between the eyebrows].* It should be a black dot;
you should not use any other colour. Then look at the
mark. First look at it with your eyes wide open, and
then gradually, gradually, close your eyes, but not
totally. Try to see the black dot with the least vision of
your human eyes. Make your eyes as wide as possible
and then immediately try to make them as tiny as
possible, so your vision is next to nothing. Then repeat
this again.

After you have succeeded in this, keep your eyes
open and try to feel that you are drilling a hole into
the wall and entering. Increase your determination
to pierce through the wall. In a few minutes you will
see that your body is here, but something of you has
passed through the wall to the other side. Your power
of concentration has taken you to the other side of the
wall. Feel that on this side of the wall is the body, and
on that side is the soul-power. So from your body you
look at your soul, and from your soul you look at your
body. Let the body see the soul's capacity, and let the
soul see the body's eagerness to become one with the

soul. If you can do this exercise, your power of concentration will increase immensely and most rapidly.

Breath from the dot

If you want to develop the power of concentration, then please do this. Before you concentrate, wash your face and eyes properly with cold water. Then make a black dot on the wall at eye level. Stand facing the dot, about ten inches *[25 cm]* away, and concentrate on it.

After a few minutes, try to feel that when you are breathing in, your breath is actually coming from the dot and that dot is also breathing in, getting its breath from you. Try to feel that there are two persons: you and the black dot that you have made. Your breath is coming from that dot and its breath is coming from you.

In ten minutes, if your concentration is very powerful, you will feel that your soul has left you and entered into the black dot on the wall. At this time, try to feel that you and your soul are conversing. Your soul is taking you into the soul's world for realisation, and you are bringing the soul into the physical world for manifestation. In this way you can develop your power of concentration very easily. But this method has to be practised. There are many things which are very easy with practice, but just because we do not practise them we do not get the result.

Vision and reality

Make a very small circle on the wall at eye-level, and inside it make a black dot. It should be black, not blue or red or any other colour. Then stand facing the wall, about three and a half feet *[one metre]* away, and focus your attention on the circle. Your eyes should be relaxed and half open. Let the force of your concentration come from the middle of your forehead.

After three or four minutes open your eyes fully and try to feel that, from head to foot, you are all eyes. Your whole physical existence has become nothing but vision. Then please concentrate on the dot inside the circle, and start making the object of your concentration smaller. After a few seconds try to feel that your whole body has become as tiny as this dot on the wall. Try to feel that the dot is another part of your own existence.

Then enter into the dot, pierce through it and go to the other side. From the other side of the dot, look back and see your own body. Your physical body is on one side, but on the strength of your concentration you have sent your subtle body to the other side of the dot. Through your subtle body you are seeing your physical body, and through your physical body you are seeing your subtle body.

When you began to concentrate, your physical body became all vision. At that time the dot was your reality. When you entered into the dot, then vision and reality became one. You were the vision and you yourself were also the reality. When you looked back at yourself from the dot, the process became reversed. At that time, you became the vision there, and the place to which you returned—your body—was the reality. Then, the vision and the reality became one again. When you can see the vision and reality in this way, your concentration is absolutely perfect. When your power of concentration can bring you to the other side of the point which you were calling reality, at that time your whole existence will be far beyond both vision and reality. The moment you can feel that you have transcended your vision and your reality, you will have boundless power.

Concentration-power
Is the strongest power
That silences uncomely thoughts
And wandering mind.

Stilling the mind

No matter what path you follow for meditation, the first and foremost task is to try to make the mind calm and quiet. If the mind is constantly roaming, if it is all the time a victim of merciless thoughts, then you will make no progress whatsoever. The mind has to be made calm and quiet so that when the light descends from above, you can be fully conscious of it. If you can keep your mind calm and quiet for ten or fifteen minutes, a new world will dawn within you.

During my deep meditation,
I lose all my mind's differences
The way a river loses
All its differences in the sea.

Chase away the monkey

The mind is like a monkey. If you are attacked by a monkey which constantly bites and pinches you, you have to threaten the monkey. Then each time it comes, if you strike it vehemently, eventually the monkey will feel that it is hopeless to try to bother you. You must always remain as vigilant as possible. When an undivine thought enters into your mind, immediately you will chase it away. If you are constantly vigilant, eventually these thoughts will give up and no longer come to disturb you.

The most important thing is practice. Today your mind acts like a monkey. It is knocking all the time at your heart's door and disturbing the poise of the heart. But as many times as the mind comes to you, just chase it away or deliberately place your conscious awareness on something else. If you allow it to distract you, it will only gain strength. You have to know that in this world, everybody has pride, vanity and self-esteem. So if you keep your heart's door closed each time the mind comes, if you pay no attention to the mind, then after some time the mind will find it beneath its dignity to bother you.

Grab the mind

Feel that inside the heart[1] there is something which is infinitely more powerful than the mind. Feel the soul, and bring the soul forward from the heart. Feel that there is intense power inside the soul. You may not see the soul, but bring forward your inner strength and then grab the mind. Say to the mind, "You allowed me to remain quiet for a few minutes, and I am grateful. But I am still praying and meditating, still crying for peace, light and bliss, and now you are not allowing me to continue."

Put the mind into the heart

Just grab the mind and put it into the flood of the heart. As long as it allows you to meditate, you do not have to worry. But when it starts bothering you, when it starts creating pain, that means it is resisting. It is not allowing you to receive more peace and light from Above.

The mind like a naughty child

Just grab the mind and feel that it is like a naughty child. Before, it was asleep and allowed the mother to remain silent or pray to God. But now the child is up and it wants to cause mischief. It does not want to allow the mother to aspire any further, to achieve more peace, light and bliss. So what will the mother do? The mother will threaten the child and say, "I am still praying, I am meditating. You must not bother me, you must not disturb me, or I will punish you."

Cut the thought to pieces

To make your mind vacant, you should not allow any thought to enter into your mind and take shape. Suppose a name comes. As soon as the first letter of the name appears, you kill the name. You have to make your mind vacant, as empty as possible, with your power of concentration.

Suppose a thought, or a vibration, or something else is coming. Immediately, shoot an arrow and pierce it into pieces. An idea comes, somebody's name comes, or some thought comes. Immediately, just throw it out. It must not come and enter into your mind. Before it touches your mind you have to cut it into pieces.

Inside the ocean

But if you already have thoughts and ideas within you, within your body, within your mind, then you have to meditate like this: be as relaxed as possible. Feel as if you are inside the ocean. Then absorb those thoughts and ideas so that they do not have a separate existence. They are lost in the sea. If they are already within you, throw them into the sea. If they are coming from outside, then do not allow them to enter into you. After doing this your meditation is bound to be successful.

Racing with a train, flying with a bird

20

If you have a good thought, feel that you are an express train racing on and on, or a bird flying up. If you have a divine idea, just run with it to your destination. But if wrong, false, undivine thoughts come, do not stay with them. Please discard them immediately.

Use a superior power

21

The reason that you are constantly bothered by thoughts is because you are trying to meditate inside your mind. The very nature of the mind is to welcome thoughts—good thoughts, bad thoughts, divine thoughts, undivine thoughts. If you want to control the mind with your human will, then it will be like asking a monkey or a fly not to bother you. The very nature of a monkey is to bite and pinch; the very nature of a fly is to bother people.

The mind needs a superior power to keep it quiet. This superior power is the power of the soul. You have to bring to the fore the light of the soul from inside your heart. You are the possessor of two rooms: the heart-room and the mind-room. Right now the mind-room is obscure, unlit and impure; it is unwilling to open to the light. But the heart-room is always open to the light, for that is where the soul abides. Instead of concentrating on the mind proper, if you can concentrate and meditate on the reality that is inside the heart, then this reality will come forward. Then, when you are well-established in the heart, when you are surcharged with the soul's light, at that time you can enter into the mind-room to illumine the mind.

Before meditation pray to God
To give you a silent mind.

Allow only your friends

If you want to learn meditation without going through concentration, you must feel that you are standing at the door of your inner room. When you stand at the door, you allow only your friends to enter into your room. You do not allow strangers or your enemies.

You have to welcome only good thoughts, divine thoughts. These are your true friends. Undivine thoughts, hostile thoughts, must not come into your mind. Your mind is constantly receiving thoughts, and you have to be very careful. You have to welcome only divine thoughts Then, play with these divine thoughts in the garden of your mind. Play with thoughts of divine qualities: divine love, divine power or divine peace. Then a time will come when you will see that there are no thoughts. Your entire being will be surcharged with inner Divinity.

Keep out the enemies

There are two kinds of thoughts: good thoughts and bad thoughts. One kind is healthy and one kind is unhealthy. Unhealthy thoughts, undivine thoughts, are our enemies, whereas good thoughts, divine thoughts, are our friends. We are standing at the door to our house and somebody is knocking at the door. We have to see whether it is a friend or enemy. If it is a friend, then we will allow him to enter. If it is an enemy, no, we will not allow him.

But the difficulty is that sometimes when we open the door just a little, immediately the enemies may force their way in. So what do we do? We do not open the door at all. We keep the door bolted from inside. Our real friends will not go away. They will think, "Something is wrong with him. Usually he is so kind to us. So there must be some special reason why he is not opening the door." They have sympathetic oneness, so they will wait indefinitely.

But our enemies want only to bother us, to torture and destroy us. They will wait just for a few minutes. Then they will lose all patience and say, "It is beneath our dignity to waste our time here." These enemies have their pride. They will say, "Who cares? Who needs him? Let us go and attack somebody else." If we pay no attention to a monkey, the monkey will eventually go away and bite somebody else.

But our friends will say, "No, we need him and he needs us. We will wait indefinitely for him." So after a few minutes our enemies will go away. Then we can open the door, and our dearest friends will be there waiting for us.

O my ordinary thoughts,
O my undivine, unhealthy
And uncomely thoughts,
During my meditation
If you knock at my mind's door,
This time I shall not open it,
For I know
That you will only misuse
The power of my meditation
To increase your own power.

Guard the door

To control your thoughts, feel that there is a room inside your mind, and naturally the room has a door. It is your room, so you can stand outside the door and not allow any thought to come in. You can keep the mind-room under lock and key, and stand at the door. Since it is your room, who can enter without your permission? But if you leave the door open, anybody can come in, and once they are inside it is difficult for you to throw them out. So you have to prevent them from coming in.

Give thoughts a human form

Now let us take a thought. You will say that naturally you concentrate only on good thoughts. But unfortunately, we do unconsciously meditate on bad thoughts. Jealousy, doubt, suspicion—all these we cherish unconsciously. When this kind of bad thought comes, just think of jealousy, fear, doubt and hypocrisy as people, and immediately give them a human form: "This fellow has undivine qualities." When it is a good thought, also give it form: "This man has all good qualities—humility, sincerity and so on."

Then what do you do? When you see a good man, feel that he is leading you and try to follow him as long as he wants you to. But if you see a bad man—a man full of fear, anxiety and so forth—feel that he is going to chase you mercilessly and that you have to immediately run away from him. You must never allow him to come near you. When you see someone destructive in front of you, immediately react as though he will destroy you. Feel that your very life is in danger.

Very often in the spiritual life, people do not take bad thoughts seriously enough. We cherish these undivine qualities and feel that they are only insects pinching us. But when you have these undivine qualities, you have to feel that they are worse than dragons, something very dangerous.

You are God's child

You can begin by having good thoughts: "I want to be good. I want to be more spiritual. I want to love God more, I want to exist only for Him." Let these ideas grow within you. Start with one or two divine ideas: "Today I want to feel that I am really a child of God." This is not a mere feeling, but an actual reality. Feel that the Virgin Mary is holding the child Christ. Feel that the Divine Mother is holding you in her arms like a baby. Then feel: "I really want to have wisdom-light. I want to walk with my Father. Wherever He goes, I will go with Him. I will get light from Him."

Put a shield in front of your forehead

Here, right in front of your forehead, you have to feel that you have a shield, right in front of you. It is a protection. Instead of taking it as a part of your body, as a limb or an organ, you have to feel that right on your forehead is a coating, a protection. Try to feel that you are constantly on the lookout, here in your mind, to see if an attack is coming, if a thought is going to attack you. At the same time, try to feel that here, in the same place, is a shield, a solid wall. This is for the thoughts that are coming from the outside.

Enlarge the good thoughts

At every moment we are assailed by bad thoughts or we are inspired by good thoughts. Each thought can act like an atom bomb in our life. When we are assailed by a bad thought, we will try to discard it. When we are assailed by a good thought, we will try to develop and enlarge it. When we start meditating early in the morning, if one good thought comes, let us enlarge it. Let us say it is a thought of divine Love—not the human, emotional love but divine, universal Love: "I love God, I love God's entire Creation."

Invoke purity

You can meditate and tell your mind, "I shall not allow you to go in your own way. Now I want to think of God." Repeat the Name of God inwardly or aloud. The next moment say, "I want to have purity in my whole existence." Then repeat 'purity, purity, purity'. At that time you are not allowing your mind to think of impurity or of some other person or thing. Do not give your mind a chance to wander: simply utilise your mind for your own purpose. You have millions of things to accomplish in and through the mind. But the mind is so naughty and mischievous that if you do not utilise it, it will utilise you.

Strangle undivine thoughts

Another way is this: when a thought comes that is not pure, good or divine, immediately repeat the word 'Supreme' very fast. The Supreme is my Guru, your Guru, everybody's Guru. So repeat 'Supreme' very fast, and each time you use the word 'Supreme', please feel that you are creating a snake that will coil around the undivine thought and strangle it. If jealousy comes, say 'Supreme' very fast, and you will see that around the jealous thought is a coil which will strangle the jealousy.

Slow down the thought-current

Every thought or idea that enters into your mind you have to silence. If you cannot silence it, then try to slow down its speed. If some current of thought is entering into you very rapidly and you cannot stop it altogether, then try at least to slow it down. And eventually you will try to silence it.

Imagine the sky or the sea

To make the mind more silent, it is good if you can imagine something very peaceful, such as the vast sky early in the morning or the setting sun in the evening. Or you can try to feel that you are at the bottom of the sea, or on the top of a mountain in the Himalayas.

Extend the body like an elastic belt

Now what about the thoughts that are already inside us, creating problems? It is very difficult, in comparison, to throw them out. But we can do it! How? Again it is through the extension of our consciousness. We have a body; inside this body are these wrong forces that have taken the form of ugly, damaging thoughts.

If we can extend our physical consciousness as we extend an elastic belt, we will feel that we are extending our whole body through the mind's conscious effort, through aspiration. We are extending, extending, extending the whole body to the Infinite. We are extending a sheet of white consciousness. The moment we feel the Infinite extending like a sheet of white consciousness, we will see that it is all purity.

Concentrate on the third eye

We have seven *chakras*[5] or spiritual centres in the body. If you want to control your thoughts, you should concentrate on the centre between the eyebrows. If you become very stiff and your concentration is intense, then you should not concentrate here for more than two minutes. Otherwise, you will become exhausted in the beginning.

Throw the mind far away

One has to see the mind as a material object. We can take a material object and put it anywhere we want to, or we can throw it the farthest possible distance, according to our strength. So either we can grab the mind like a material object and throw it into the distance, or we can put the mind wherever we want to.

Feel you are the heart

Totally forget about the existence of the mind. Ignore the mind and feel oneself only as the heart. It is not enough to say, "I have a heart." One must say, "I am the heart, I am the heart." Then the qualities of the heart will permeate the entire being, and automatically the mind will stop.

The soundless sound

If you concentrate on the heart centre[1], you will get peace, love and joy. Try to hear the cosmic sound, the *soundless sound*[6], when you enter into the heart. If you bring love, joy, peace and bliss up from the heart to the centre between the eyebrows, then you will see that there will be no thoughts.

The heart is the safest place for you to concentrate and meditate on. If you do this, automatically you will get purification, because inside the heart is the soul, and the soul is one with the Infinite. It is from here that you will get everything.

Two meditation secrets:
Safest is the heart centre,
Fastest is the crown centre.

Breathing
exercises

Breathing exercises are of real help to meditation. If we do breathing exercises for five or ten minutes first, it will be of great help to our meditation. While you are breathing you have to imagine and feel that an abundance of life-energy is entering into you. Life-energy is nothing but aspiration—our inner cry for Light, Love and Happiness.

Do you want to be happy?
Then make your life
As soulfully simple
As sleeplessly breathing.

Thread in front of the nose

Proper breathing is very important in meditation. When breathing, try to breathe in as slowly and quietly as possible, so that if somebody placed a tiny thread in front of your nose, it would not move at all. And when you breathe out, try to breathe out even more slowly than when you breathed in. If possible, leave a short pause between the end of your first exhalation and the beginning of your second inhalation. If you can, hold your breath for a few seconds. But if it is difficult, do not do it. Never do anything that will harm your organs or respiratory system.

Breathe through different parts of your body

Before you start meditating, please breathe in deeply a few times. With each breath, try to feel that a stream of energy is entering into you. Then try to feel that you are breathing in through different parts of your body: your eyes, your ears, your forehead, your shoulders, the crown of your head and so on. Feel that each of these places is a door, and when you breathe in, feel that you are opening this door. At that time, energy enters in from the Universal Consciousness.

Life-energy in the chakras

40

Please breathe in and hold the breath in the *third eye*[3] for a couple of seconds. Your concentration will be in the *third eye*. The second time you breathe in, hold the life-energy in the heart centre[1]. You are holding the breath, the life-energy, here. The third time you breathe in, hold the breath in the navel. Please repeat this, first in the *third eye*, then in the heart, then in the navel.

Your breath is God's playground

41

Try to feel that your heart is a vast playground, and that inside this playground there is a special and sacred place where God likes to play. That chosen place is inside your life-breath. Each time you breathe in or breathe out, try to feel that the breath you are inhaling or exhaling is for God. When you are breathing in good thoughts, you have to feel that those good thoughts are for God. And when you are breathing out undivine thoughts, you have to feel that those undivine thoughts are also for God. You do not have to count how many good thoughts you have breathed in or how many bad thoughts you have breathed out. No! Only you have to remember that, good or bad, each breath of yours is for God only.

Seven higher worlds

While breathing in, with each breath try to repeat 'Supreme'[2] slowly seven times and again seven times while breathing out. Inside you there are seven higher worlds and seven lower worlds. When you repeat 'Supreme' while breathing in, feel that you are going into the seven higher worlds inside you. Once you have reached the seven higher worlds, you will find solid power. When you breathe out, think of the seven lower worlds within you and try to throw the strength of the higher worlds into the lower worlds. Accumulate everything in the higher worlds and then, while saying 'Supreme, Supreme, Supreme...' when you are breathing out, enter into the lower worlds with peace, light and bliss to purify the lower worlds.

Breathe in purity

The first thing that you have to think of when breathing is purity. When you breathe in, if you can feel that the breath is coming directly from God, from Purity itself, then your breath can easily be purified.

Breathe in power and joy

Please try to feel that you are breathing in power from the universe. And when you exhale, feel that all your fear is coming out of your body. After doing this a few times, try to feel that what you are breathing in is joy, infinite joy, and what you are breathing out is sorrow, suffering and melancholy.

Breathe in peace, breathe out restlessness

45 Each time you breathe in, try to feel that you are bringing into your body peace, infinite peace. The opposite of peace is restlessness. When you breathe out, try to feel that you are expelling the restlessness within you and also the restlessness that you see all around you. When you breathe this way, you will find restlessness leaving you.

Cosmic energy

46 Feel that you are breathing in not air but cosmic energy. Feel that tremendous cosmic energy is entering into you with each breath and that you are going to use it to purify your body, vital[9], mind and heart. Feel that there is not a single place in your body that is not being occupied by the flow of cosmic energy. It is flowing like a river inside you, washing and purifying your whole being.

Then, when you start to breathe out, feel that you are breathing out all the rubbish inside you—all your undivine thoughts, obscure ideas and impure actions. Anything inside your system that you call undivine, anything that you do not want to claim as your own, feel that you are exhaling.

One-four-two breathing

We have a traditional system of controlled breathing in India which is called *pranayama*, control of the life-breath. *Prana* is the vital energy, the life-breath; *yama* means control. The very first exercise you can practise is to repeat once, as you breathe in, the Name of God, the Christ or whomever you adore. Or, if your Master has given you a mantra, you can repeat that. This breath does not have to be long or deep.

Then hold your breath and repeat the same name four times. And when you breathe out, repeat two times the name or mantra that you have chosen. You inhale for one count, hold your breath for four counts, and exhale for two counts, inwardly repeating the sacred name. If you simply count the numbers—one-four-two—you do not get any vibration or inner feeling. But when you say the Name of God, immediately God's divine qualities enter into you. Then, when you hold your breath, these divine qualities rotate inside you, entering into all your impurities, obscurities, imperfections and limitations. And when you breathe out, these same divine qualities carry away all your undivine, unprogressive and destructive qualities.

The beginner starts with a one-four-two count. When he becomes mature in his breathing, he will be able to do it to a count of four-sixteen-eight: breathing in for four counts, holding the breath for sixteen, and breathing out for eight. But this has to be done very gradually. Some people even do this with an eight–thirty-two–sixteen count, but this is not for the beginner.

Alternate nostril breathing

Another thing you can try is alternate breathing. This is done by pressing the right nostril with the thumb and taking in a long breath through the left nostril. As you breathe in, repeat God's Name once. Then hold your breath for four counts, repeating God's Name four times. And finally release your right nostril, press your left nostril with your fourth finger and release your breath to the count of two—that is, two repetitions of God's Name. Then do it the opposite way, starting with the left nostril pressed closed. In this system, when you breathe in, it does not have to be done quietly. Even if you make a noise, no harm. But, of course, these exercises should not be done in public or where other people are trying to meditate in silence.

You should not practise one-four-two breathing for more than four or five minutes, and you should not do alternate breathing more than three times. If you do it twenty or forty or fifty times, heat will rise from the base of your spine and enter into your head, creating tension and a headache. It is like eating too much. Eating is good, but if you eat voraciously, it will upset your stomach. This heat acts the same way. If you draw it up beyond your capacity, then instead of giving you a peaceful mind, it will give you an arrogant, turbulent and destructive mind. Later, when you have developed your inner capacity, you can do this alternate breathing for ten or fifteen minutes.

Pranayama is a traditional yogic discipline with many serious, complicated breathing exercises. They can be dangerous if they are not done properly or if you do not have a teacher to guide you at every step. But these exercises that I am telling you about—the one-four-two count and alternate nostril breathing— are very simple and, at the same time, effective. They will never harm your lungs.

I meditate
So that I can consecrate
Each breath of mine
To better human life.

Mantras

A mantra is an incantation. It can be a syllable, a word, a few words or a sentence. When you repeat a mantra many times, it is called japa. A mantra represents a particular aspect of God, and each mantra has a special significance and inner power.

If you cannot enter into your deepest meditation because your mind is restless, this is an opportunity to utilise a mantra. By repeating a mantra we can bring to the fore our own inner divinity.

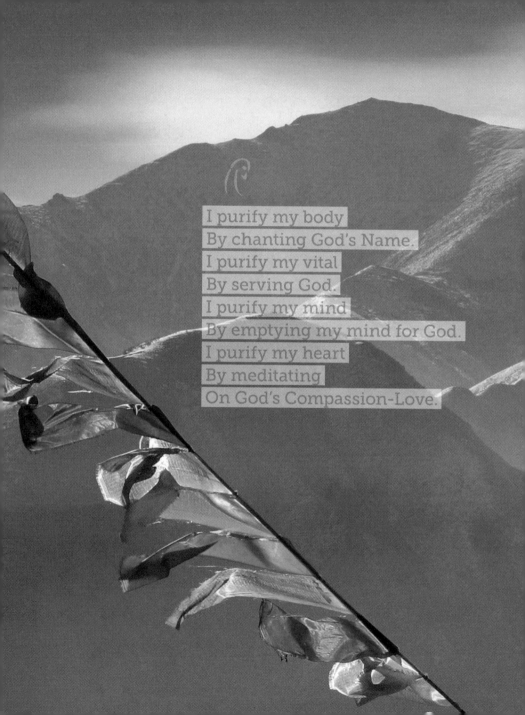

I purify my body
By chanting God's Name.
I purify my vital
By serving God.
I purify my mind
By emptying my mind for God.
I purify my heart
By meditating
On God's Compassion-Love.

How to stop the mind

There are quite a few ways to stop the mind. One way is to repeat the Name of God or a particular mantra, which is a sacred word or incantation. When we repeat a mantra or God's Name, there is a continuous flow. If what we are repeating is 'God, God, God', then inside the repetition itself we will forget ourselves and lose ourselves. Then the mind stops.

Repeating divine qualities

Please inwardly repeat the word 'love, love, love' most soulfully. While uttering 'love' most soulfully, please try to feel that this word is reverberating in the inmost recesses of your heart: 'love, love, love'.

If you care more for the concept of peace, divine peace, then please chant the word 'peace' inwardly, or repeat it to yourself. Try to hear the sound, the cosmic sound that embodies that word. The word 'peace' will be a seed-sound reverberating in the very depths of your heart. If you want light, then please repeat the word 'light, light, light.' While uttering the word, chanting or soulfully repeating it, please feel that you have become that word or divine quality. Feel that your very existence, from the sole of your foot to the crown of your head, has become love, or the quality you are repeating. All your nerves, your subtle body, your physical body, everything, everything is flooded with love. The quality has that magic power. Love, peace, light, delight: you choose the divine quality which you wish to embody and become.

Repeat 'Aum' or 'Supreme'

If you cannot enter into your deepest meditation because your mind is restless, this is an opportunity to utilise a mantra. You can repeat 'Supreme'[2] or 'Aum'[6] or 'God' for a few minutes.

Loudly or softly

There are many ways to chant *Aum*. If you chant it loudly, you feel the Omnipotence of the Supreme. When you chant it softly, you feel the Delight of the Supreme. When you chant it silently, you feel the Peace of the Supreme. When we chant *Aum* with tremendous soul's power, what we actually do is enter into the cosmic vibration where the creation is in perfect harmony and where the cosmic Dance is being danced by the Absolute.

Please practise it aloud, not silently. Let the sound of the mantra vibrate even in your physical ears and permeate your entire body. This will convince your outer mind and give you a greater sense of joy and achievement. When chanting out loud, the '*m*' sound should last at least three times as long as the '*Au*' sound.

Life-energy entering the crown chakra

When you chant *Aum*, please feel that life-energy, divine energy, is entering into you through your crown centre. The breath that you breathe in through the nose is very limited; but if you can imagine that there is a big hole in the top of your head and that life-energy, cosmic energy, is entering into your body through that big hole, then naturally you will be able to accelerate your purification and increase your aspiration and hunger for God, truth, light and bliss.

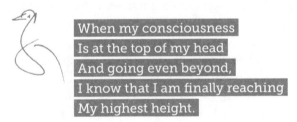

When my consciousness
Is at the top of my head
And going even beyond,
I know that I am finally reaching
My highest height.

Total purification

If you want to achieve overall purification of your nature, then *japa*[8] *[repetition of a mantra]* can be most effective. But you have to do it in a systematic way, step by step. Today repeat '*Aum*' or 'Supreme' or whatever mantra your Master has given you five hundred times. Then tomorrow repeat it six hundred times, the day after tomorrow, seven hundred, and so on, until you reach twelve hundred in one week's time. Then begin descending each day until you reach five hundred again. In this way you can climb up the tree and climb down the tree.

Please continue this exercise, week by week, for a month. Whether you want to change your name or not, the world will give you a new name: 'Purity'.

Japa in small segments

55

If it is difficult for you to do this exercise at one stretch, then you can do it in pieces. You can do it ten times; each time you will repeat the mantra only fifty times. You know that during the day you want to drink ten glasses of water. But if you drink all ten glasses of water at once, you are afraid it will upset your stomach; so you will not drink them all at once. But if you drink one glass now, and then after an interval of an hour or two, another glass, easily you can drink ten glasses of water.

So here also, instead of chanting 'Aum' five hundred times all at once, early in the morning you can repeat it fifty times. Then, in an hour's time, you try another fifty. So each hour if you repeat 'Aum' fifty times, each time it will not take you more than a minute or two. Since you can easily spend two minutes in an hour, you can do it.

If you have a mantra or incantation of your own, you can easily do it fifty times an hour. It cannot take more than two or three minutes, and everyone can offer three minutes to God. It is not how many hours you can do it at a time that is important, but how soulfully you can do it.

As fast as possible

If you get an attack on the emotional vital[9] plane and wrong thoughts or wrong vibrations are entering into you, you can repeat 'Aum' or the Name of the Supreme. In this case try to do it as fast as possible. When you are trying to cleanse your mind of impurities, you must chant as if you were running to catch a moving train. During regular *japa*, however, just say the mantra in a normal but soulful way, but do not prolong it too much; otherwise, you will not have time to chant the five hundred or six hundred times that are necessary.

Chanting your spiritual name

I do not emphasise the importance of mantras for those following my path. But if a student of mine does want to practise a mantra, I tell him that he can repeat the Name of God—'Supreme'[2]—or he can chant 'Aum'. Again, if he does not care to repeat these divine words, he can chant his own soul's name. To some students I have given spiritual names, soul's names. If you can repeat your own soul's name, I assure you that you will be able to bring to the fore all your divine qualities and to become energised with divine power. If you repeat even ten times very slowly the spiritual name I have given you, then a new and fruitful consciousness will dawn in you.

The Gayatri mantra

In the Bhagavad Gita[10], Sri Krishna says that the Gayatri mantra is the best of all the mantras:

Aum bhūr bhuvaḥ svaḥ
Tat savitur vareṇyam
Bhargo devasya dhīmahi
Dhiyo yo naḥ pracodayāt
(Rigveda III.62.10)

We meditate on the transcendental glory
of the Deity Supreme,
Who is inside the heart of the earth,
Inside the life of the sky,
And inside the soul of the Heaven.
May He stimulate and illumine our minds.

By repeating this mantra, hundreds and hundreds of seekers have attained to spiritual perfection. If you can repeat it soulfully thousands of times at a stretch, you are bound to get at least an iota of inner illumination. But it has to be done most soulfully, and not like a child learning something by rote.

TIP

If you received your mantra, *japa* and meditation all from the same Master, you should practise them at three different times of the day, because the forces of these practices do not go together. In the morning, if you want to, you can chant a specific mantra, in the evening you can do *japa* and at some other time you can do meditation. Otherwise, while you are meditating, if you suddenly get the inspiration to do *japa* or to chant some specific mantra, you will only ruin your aspiration. *Japa* and mantras have their own significant power, but in the highest type of meditation, when your inner being is communing with God, at that time there is no thought, no idea; your mind is calm and quiet, so there should be no mantra or *japa* there.

If you make a mistake
In spite of your best intentions,
Remember this mantra:
"The past is dust."

Mantric songs

59

Singing immediately inspires us and awakens the slumbering soul in us. If we sing a divine song, a soulful song, it immediately brings purity into our system. Singing purifies our limited consciousness and brings to us universal Harmony. In our day-to-day life, we constantly break the universal Harmony, but when we sing, we build and create this universal Harmony in and around us.

If we can sing, we can have the purest consciousness and perfect harmony in our nature. Nothing delights our soul more than soulful singing.

When we chant, our psychic being, which is the representative of the soul, is fed. A mother feeds her child whenever the child is hungry. Similarly, we have to feed the soul, the divine child within us, by chanting or meditating. When the soul is constantly fed, it comes to the fore and the soul-bird gets the opportunity to fly in the sky of Infinity and Eternity.

*Note: Some of the following mantras are in original English, other in Bengali or Sanskrit. You can find a few guides to the pronunciation in the back of this book. You can download the recordings of the mantras on **www.101.......***

Gayatri mantra

Words: Sanskrit mantra
Music: Sri Chinmoy, 1982

♩ = 63 *Moderate-slow*

Aum   bhur   bhu – vah   svah____

Tat   sa – – – vi – tur____   va – ren – – – – yam

Bhar – go   de – vas – – – ya   dhi – ma – – – hi

Dhi – yo   yo nah____   pra – – cho – da – – – yat

We meditate on the transcendental glory
of the Deity Supreme,
Who is inside the heart of the earth,
Inside the life of the sky,
And inside the soul of the Heaven.
May He stimulate and illumine our minds.

Mantras for protection, transformation, victory and delight

Words: sanskrit mantras
Music: Sri Chinmoy, 1982

Aum Go - vin - da - ya na - ma____

Aum. I bow to Lord Govinda. (for divine protection*)

Aum____ Ru - - dra - - ya na - - - - - ma

Aum. I bow to Lord Rudra. (for spiritual transformation*)

Aum A-pa-ra - ji - - ta - - ya na - - - - - - - - ma

Aum. I bow to the Lord who never accepts defeat.
(for victory and never giving up*)

Aum___ Am - - - ri - - - ta - - ya na - - - - ma

Aum. I bow to the Lord of Nectar. (for joy and nectar-delight*)

* editor's note

Chanchala man

Words and music: Sri Chinmoy
1977

$\quad$ = 116 Moderate-fast

Chăn - chă - lă măn   du - re   rā - khi   chăn - chă - lă   mor   măn

Chăn - chă - lă măn   du - re   rā - khi   chăn - chă - lă   mor   măn

I keep aside my restless mind,
Always I keep it aside.

Meditation

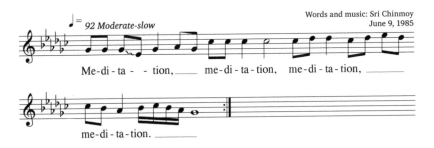

Words and music: Sri Chinmoy
June 9, 1985

$\quad$ = 92 Moderate-slow

Me - di - ta - - tion, _____ me - di - ta - tion,   me - di - ta - tion, _____

me - di - ta - tion. _____

Shanti (Peace)

Words and music: Sri Chinmoy
October 17, 1989

Moderate

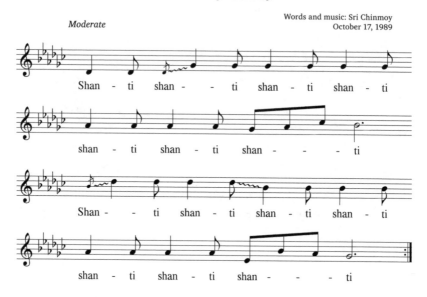

Shan - ti shan - - ti shan - ti shan - ti

shan - ti shan - ti shan - - - ti

Shan - - ti shan - ti shan - ti shan - ti

shan - ti shan - ti shan - - - ti

Habo ami

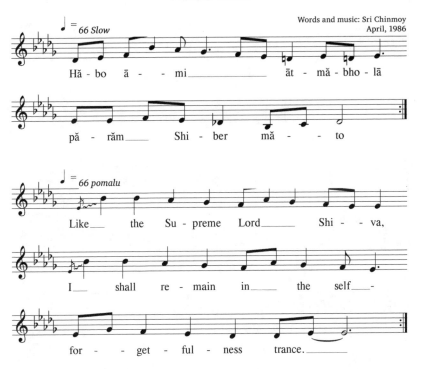

Words and music: Sri Chinmoy
April, 1986

Hă - bo ā - - mi_____ āt - mă - bho - lā

pă - răm___ Shi - ber mă - - to

Like___ the Su - preme Lord___ Shi - - va,

I___ shall re - main in___ the self___-

for - - get - ful - ness trance.___

Like the Supreme Lord Shiva,
I shall remain in the self-forgetfulness trance.

Supreme Chant

Opening the heart

The spiritual heart is located right in the centre of the chest. It houses all the divine qualities. Our soul abides in the spiritual heart. When the heart centre actually opens, its joy and delight spread to the whole body.

The spiritual heart is vaster than the vastest. Right now, Infinity is an imaginary concept for us. But when we discover our inner heart, our spiritual heart, Infinity is no longer imagination; it is reality.

What do I see in my meditation?
In my meditation I see
A larger-than-the-largest
Ocean of peace
And blue-vast sky
Inside my tinier-than-the-tiniest
Heart.

Feel like a child

For a beginner to meditate in the heart, he has to feel that he is a child, no matter how old he is in earthly age. A child's mind is not developed. When he is twelve or thirteen, his mind starts functioning on an intellectual level, but before that he is all heart. Whatever he sees, he feels is his own. He identifies spontaneously. This is what the heart does.

Play in a flower garden

When you feel that you are a child, immediately feel that you are standing in a flower garden. This flower garden is your heart. A child can play in a garden for hours. He will go from this flower to that flower, but he will not leave the garden, because he will get joy from the beauty and fragrance of each flower. Inside you is the garden, and you can stay within it for as long as you want. In this way you can meditate on the heart.

Cry like a helpless child

A child will always have someone to take care of him even if his physical parents are not there. God will have somebody to take care of the child, because He feels that the child is helpless right now. When a child cries, immediately someone comes to help him. When

a child cries even for a candy, he is very sincere. At that time his candy is the whole world for him. If you give him a hundred-dollar bill, he will not be satisfied; he will only care for his candy. When you feel you are crying like a child for peace, light and truth, and that only those things will satisfy you, then your cry will be fulfilled.

A flower blossoming in the heart

63   When you meditate, please meditate on the heart, and then try to have the peace, light and bliss of the heart percolate through the entire being. In the heart you have peace, and like a flower it has to blossom petal by petal, here, there, everywhere. Then you have a flower of peace whose petals have blossomed in all parts of the being.

Concentrate on your heart

64   If you can concentrate on the tip of your finger, or on a candle or any other material object, you can also concentrate on your heart. You may close your eyes or look at a wall, but all the time you are thinking of your heart as a dear friend. When this thinking becomes most intense, when it absorbs your entire at-

tention, then you have gone beyond ordinary thinking and entered into concentration. You cannot look physically at your spiritual heart[1], but you can focus all your attention on it. Then gradually the power of your concentration enters into the heart and takes you completely out of the realm of the mind.

Consciousness of the heart

When you start your morning meditation, you have to feel that you *have* the heart and that you *are* the heart. Then, after some time, your consciousness will tell you where the heart is. At that time, you will concentrate on that spot and feel that that is the only place for you to *become* the heart.

Concentrate and meditate on purity.
Lo, all your inner resistance disappears
And automatically your heart's door
Is wide open.

Feel your heartbeat

66

If you keep your hands on top of your heart and feel your heartbeat, automatically you will feel the intensity of your aspiration. Inside that intensity you will discover the purity of your mind and the divinity of your heart.

Invite your friends into your heart

67

Please feel that you are standing at your heart's door and you have invited your friends, love, peace, light, delight, power, and other friends that you cherish and treasure, to enter. If every day you can invite even one friend, it will be the beginning of a divine friendship. Say to yourself, "Today I will allow only my friend love to come in and not anybody else. Tomorrow I will allow my friend joy to come in and the day after tomorrow I will invite my friend peace to come in."

Then you may say, "I have developed considerably. I have the capacity to invite more than one friend in. I shall definitely invite all my friends in—love, joy, peace, light and delight. But I did not have enough means to feed more than one friend at a time, therefore I could only invite one friend. Now I can invite all my divine friends and allow them to enter into my heart-room."

You are nothing but your heart

68

Feel that you have no arms, no nose, no eyes, no ears; you do not have anything but the heart. This heart need not be in the centre of your chest; it may be in your forehead or somewhere else.

Try to feel that all your strength, all your determination and will-power, is in one particular place, here inside your heart. Feel that you do not exist at all except in this tiny place. You do not have eyes, you do not have a nose, you do not have anything else. Intensity will come only when you feel that your entire existence is concentrated at one particular place and not scattered.

Look at your heart in a mirror

69

If you get a strange feeling like tension in your head, please feel that you do not have a head or a forehead; only feel that you have a heart. You have this tension because you are meditating in the wrong place. You are meditating inside the mind, which is not advisable. Try to focus all your attention on your heart. You can even keep a mirror in front of you, and look at your own heart that way if you find it difficult to concentrate inwardly on your heart.

Concentrate on your Master's heart

Another thing you can do is look at a picture of your spiritual Master and, instead of looking at his *third eye*, look at his heart. Either concentrate on your own heart, with or without a mirror, or look at his picture and feel his heart—whichever way pleases you.

The shrine in your heart

If you do not have purity in abundant measure, if countless earthly desires are in possession of the heart, then before concentrating on the heart you should invoke purity. Purity is the feeling of having a living shrine deep in the inmost recesses of your heart. When you feel the divine presence of an inner shrine, automatically you are purified. At that time your concentration on the heart will be most effective.

Purity in the heart

We can have more heart-power by repeating, "I am the heart, I am the heart, I am not the mind." The qualities of heart-power are purity, beauty and the feeling of oneness. When we think of a temple, immediately we think of the shrine inside it. We think of the flowers, incense and so forth on the shrine.

Otherwise, a temple is like any other building. But when we say 'temple', immediately inside our body, inside our nerves, inside our being, we feel something pure. Something is elevating our consciousness. What is it? It is the candles, the incense and the flowers on the shrine. Anything that deals with purity we think of at that time.

In exactly the same way, when we think of heart-power, the most significant treasure that the heart has is purity. When you think of the mind, purity is not to be found there. At that time, you only think of confusion or supremacy: the mind is either thinking that you are useless, or that the rest of the world is jealous of you. There is nobody to feel or establish oneness with the mind. The good qualities of the mind are serenity, clarity and illumination. But these are rarely found.

A flower in your heart

When you think of heart-power, the first thing you have to think of is purity-power. What gives us an immediate sense of purity? Any flower that you like best—a rose or lotus or some other flower. You have to feel that you are breathing in the beauty and fragrance of the flower that you like most. Please try to visualise it inside your heart.

First feel that the flower is there. Imagine it inside your heart. Imagination has a reality of its own. As soon as you imagine that there is a flower inside you, a rose or any other flower, then try to smell the fragrance of that flower.

Then, after fifteen minutes or half an hour or even a few days, try to feel that that flower has become invisible inside your heart. You do not have to see the flower as such, you do not have to smell the fragrance, no. As soon as you think of your heart, you will see that your heart has become the most beautiful flower, the most beautiful rose.

So in order to acquire heart-power or to be conscious of heart-power, we first have to develop purity-power. And inside purity is oneness. Purity accepts everybody. A child is pure; that is why a child accepts everyone. A flower is pure; it allows everyone to appreciate its beauty.

When we look at a flower,
We get the fragrance of the flower.
Lo, for a few seconds
Our consciousness ascends
And we become self-giving.

The sun rising in your heart

74

No matter what time of the day you are meditating, even if it is in the evening, imagine the rising sun for a few fleeting seconds. Imagine that the sun is rising and radiating light inside your heart. Or you can imagine a most beautiful and most pure flower opening up and blossoming petal by petal inside your heart.

As soon as you see either the rising sun or the flower, you will feel the light or the purity of your heart. Then, as you breathe in and breathe out, you will feel the light or purity inside your heart increase. And the more light and purity you feel in your heart, the brighter will be the rising sun or the flower. Afterwards, try to feel that you have become the rising sun. Or try to feel that the purity-flower inside your heart has fully blossomed and that you have become this most beautiful flower. Your very existence, from the soles of your feet to the crown of your head, is the flower itself. The beauty, the purity, the fragrance of the flower is all you.

From the rising sun or the most beautiful flower that you have become, light will radiate and purity will spread. When the light and purity spread, they enter into those around you. In this way you can meditate more in the heart. Do not feel that you have to *go* to the heart. Only feel that you *are* the heart.

75

The garden in your heart

Inside our heart-garden are all our divine qualities. They are like beautiful and fragrant flowers. First, repeat to yourself, "I am inside my heart-garden." Try to see and feel all the beautiful flowers there. Then say, "I am my heart-garden. All the divine flowers inside my heart-garden are part and parcel of my own self." Up until now you have established your oneness with the reality that you see in your outer life. But now you want to establish your oneness with the dearest and purest existence of yours, which is your inner life, the life of your heart.

When you are meditating, if you happen to look at your shoulder or your knee, please say to yourself, "This is my heart." If you have a good thought during your meditation, then immediately inside that good thought try to feel the existence of your heart.

Every day
When you meditate,
Try to feel that your life
Is in your heart's
Fragrance-garden.

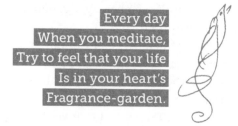

Visualisations

Visualisation connects the power of concentration with the power of imagination. Imagination is of paramount importance. Scientists, poets — not to speak of Yogis — have all come to realise that imagination is the precursor of reality. What we call imagination is nothing short of reality in some other plane of consciousness. Today we imagine something and tomorrow that very thing is transformed into reality by virtue of our aspiration.

From tomorrow on
My morning meditation
Will be as beautiful as the dawn,
My midday meditation,
As powerful as the sun
And my evening meditation,
As peaceful as the sky.

A rose blossoming in the heart

Kindly imagine a flower inside your heart, a rose. Feel that the rose is not fully blossomed; it is in a bud form. After you have meditated for two or three minutes, please try to imagine that petal by petal the rose is blossoming. See and feel the rose blossoming petal by petal inside your heart.

Then, after five minutes, try to feel that there is no heart at all; there is only a flower inside you called 'heart'. You do not have a heart, but only a flower. The flower has become your heart or your heart has become a flower.

After seven or eight minutes, please feel that the flower-heart or heart-flower has covered your whole body. Your body is no longer here; from your head to your feet you feel the fragrance of the rose. If you look at your feet, immediately you feel the fragrance of a rose. If you look at your knee, you feel the fragrance of a rose. If you look at your head, you feel the fragrance of a rose. Everywhere you feel the rose. The beauty and the fragrance and the light of the rose have permeated your whole body.

When you feel from your head to your feet that you have become only the beauty, fragrance, light and delight of the rose, then you are ready to place yourself at the Feet of the Beloved Supreme, who is my Guru⁴, your Guru, everybody's Guru. You feel, "Lord Supreme, now I place myself at Your Feet." Then your meditation is over.

The vastness of the ocean

When you want to meditate, at that time think of something very vast—the sky, the ocean, the mountains—and become one with the vastness, which is all power.

Imagine something very vast, calm and quiet. When you start meditating, feel that inside you is a vast ocean and that you have dived to the bottom, where it is all tranquillity. If you can identify yourself with this vast ocean, with this flood of tranquillity, then it will be extremely easy for you to meditate.

Bottom of the sea

Meditation is like going to the bottom of the sea, where everything is calm and tranquil. On the surface there may be a multitude of waves, but the sea is not affected below. In its deepest depths, the sea is all silence. When we start meditating, first we try to reach our own inner existence, our true existence—that is to say, the bottom of the sea.

Then, when the waves come from the outside world, we are not affected. Fear, doubt, worry and all the earthly turmoil will just wash away, because inside us is solid peace. Thoughts cannot touch us, because our mind is all peace, all silence, all oneness. Like fish in the sea, they jump and swim but leave no mark. So when we are in our highest meditation, we feel that we are the sea, and the animals in the sea cannot affect us. We feel that we are the sky, and all the birds flying past cannot affect us. Our mind is the sky and our heart is the infinite sea. This is meditation.

Vastness of the sky

Kindly keep your eyes half open and imagine the vast sky. In the beginning try to feel that the sky is in front of you; later try to feel that you are as vast as the sky, or that you are the vast sky itself.

After a few minutes, please close your eyes and try to see and feel the sky inside your heart. Please feel that you are the Universal Heart, and that inside you is the sky that you meditated upon and identified yourself with. Your spiritual heart is infinitely vaster than the sky, so you can easily house the sky within yourself.

Let the river flow through you

When you meditate, please try to feel the river of meditation flowing through you without coercion or exertion. Let the divine consciousness flow through you. That flow is the real meditation which you have had many, many times. You can always have the real meditation if you allow the river of consciousness to flow in and through you.

Let this energy, which comes in a very exuberant way, flow from the soles of your feet to the crown of your head like a river. Do not try to hold it. Let it not be accumulated at one particular place. Let it take the form of liquid energy. You will see that automatically you will become calm and quiet again. By consciously trying to help the energy flow from one place to another inside you, you will be able to enjoy that divine energy.

The rising sun

In India seekers get up at the Hour of God, three o'clock in the morning, and start to meditate on the rising sun. The sun represents dynamism, inner beauty and inner light. The sun is a manifestation of God's transcendence. As the flower is God's outer manifestation of beauty and purity, the sun is the inner manifestation of the beauty and power of God.

Light flowing like a river

Right after meditation you have to feel that the light from the heart is like a river that is flowing to all the parts of the being. The consciousness-water, the consciousness-river, has found a way to flow most satisfactorily into the other parts of the being. So there will be no fear at all. At that time you will feel a connecting link between the heart and the other parts of the being.

A white column of light

Please try to feel a white column of light coming up from your heart centre. Imagine that this white column of light has pierced the top of your head and is stationed three inches above you. Now you can start meditating. After a while try to feel that you are nothing other than that light. Feel that it is absolutely your own existence. When you feel it as your own existence, all your problems will be unmistakably solved.

Beyond speech and mind,
Into the river of ever-effulgent light
My heart dives.
Today thousands of doors, closed for millennia,
Are opened wide.

The full moon
and the new moon

When you meditate on the full moon, feel that your consciousness is fully blossomed inside you. The lotus has many petals. So think of a lotus fully blossomed inside you. You can appreciate the beauty of the fully-blossomed lotus. When you meditate on the new moon, at that time you have to feel that one petal has opened, and there are many more petals to be blossomed. Here again you get joy because when one petal of a flower is blossomed, you have the hope that tomorrow another petal will open, and the day after tomorrow, another. In that way you will see the gradual progress. Once you see some progress, you feel it will soon be complete. The full moon gives you joy from completion, and the new moon gives you joy from seeing gradual progress.

Meditate on nature

The best way to appreciate nature's beauty is to sit and meditate with nature. If you take a tree as nature, then sit at the foot of a tree and meditate. If you take the sun as an expression of nature, then look at the sun and meditate. If you feel the ocean or sea as nature, then sit in front of the water and meditate. While looking at the tree or the sun or the ocean, try to feel your oneness with it. Anything that you consider as nature or nature's beauty, you should try to become one with.

Again, if you want a particular thing from nature, you have to go to that thing. If you want to have vastness, then just go out of the house and look at the sky and you will enter into vastness. If you want to have a very vast, pure consciousness, then stand in front of a river and meditate on the river. And if you want to achieve height in your life, then go to a mountain and meditate there. If you want to meditate on the power aspect of life, then look at the sun and meditate. The sun represents power, not the power that destroys, but the power that creates, originates. And if you want to have mildness, softness, tenderness in your life, then you can meditate on the moon.

So whatever you want, you have to stand in front of that particular thing and invoke it. You have to invoke the spirit of nature or become one with the soul of nature. That is the best kind of identification.

God's Heart and God's Lap

Every day when you meditate, try to feel that you are inside the Heart of God, the Inner Pilot. Although you have not seen the Supreme, just mentally imagine a human being who is absolutely golden. Imagine that He is right in front of you and you are inside His Heart or in His Lap or at His Feet. Do not think that you are eighteen or forty or sixty years old. No! Think that you are only one month old and that you are inside the very Heart of the Supreme or in His Lap.

The Golden Being

To contemplate, try to imagine a Golden Being, and feel that He is infinitely more beautiful than the most beautiful child that you have ever seen on earth. This Being is your Beloved Lord Supreme. You are a divine lover and the Golden Being is your Beloved Lord Supreme.

Now, try to imagine that your own existence and also that of your Beloved are on the top of a mountain in the Himalayas or at the very bottom of the Pacific Ocean, whichever is easier for you. Once you feel this, then in silence you smile.

Then, after a few seconds, please feel that you yourself are the Beloved Supreme and that the Golden Being is the divine lover. It is like a game of divine hide-and-seek. When you become the Supreme Beloved, the divine lover seeks you, and when you become the divine lover, you search for your Beloved Supreme. So one moment you are the supreme lover and the next moment you are the Supreme Lord. In the beginning, please do this with your eyes half open. Later, if you wish, you can close your eyes.

Guided meditations

During our meditation,
There is an unseen friend
Who is helping
And guiding us:
Our soul.

Peace

At the top of the head is the crown centre—'*Sahasrara chakra*' we call it. Imagine that this centre is opening up seven times—imagine, but do not count them. Each time it opens, it rotates one full circle. While it is rotating, chant either 'peace' or '*Aum*'[6] or 'Supreme'[2], or you can try two of the three.

Light

At the *third eye*[3] try to imagine a disc. Imagine that the disc is rotating clockwise, and seven times chant 'light' or '*Aum*' or 'Supreme', whichever you want.

Then inside that rotating disc please imagine seven very, very bright flames. Try to imagine playing with those seven flames, and at times try to feel that you have become one with those tiny flames, instead of playing with them.

Delight

Please imagine a disc rotating around your heart centre. Now you will chant 'delight' or '*Aum*' or 'Supreme'. Inside that circle, which is the heart centre—*Anahata*, where the soundless sound comes from—please imagine that your heart is a flower-garden, absolutely larger than the largest. Inside that large garden try

to see a most beautiful swimming pool, very big. The water of the swimming pool is silver. There you are swimming, diving and doing all sorts of things that give you joy. Then see inside the swimming pool a golden boat. Enter into the golden boat, and while you are entering it, please try to imagine that your entire being has become totally golden.

FOR SEEKERS BELOW THIRTY YEARS OF AGE

Today we shall do a special type of meditation. We shall focus our attention on various places.

Jasmine in the navel

It will be safe and wise to start with the navel area[11]. So for a few seconds please meditate on the navel area and imagine a jasmine flower. The jasmine flower signifies purity. Jasmine flowers will help us purify our impure body-reality.

Lotus in the heart

Then come to the heart centre and there imagine a beautiful lotus. The beauty and the fragrance of the lotus will help us identify ourselves with the soul.

Rose in the mind

When we focus our concentration inside the mind, inside the head, kindly imagine a beautiful rose. The beauty and fragrance of the rose will help us to illumine our unlit human life.

Conch in the crown centre

Then come to the top of the head and imagine a conch, the divine victory. When we meditate on the crown centre, it will help us to blow the conch, to sound the divine victory. Imagine that the conch is announcing the divine victory, your victory.

FOR SEEKERS OVER THIRTY YEARS OF AGE

We shall focus our concentration first on the heart, then on the third eye, and then on the top of the head.

Golden boat in the heart

Let us start with the heart. We shall imagine a golden boat inside the heart. This boat will be our Eternity's boat, our own Eternity's boat which is sailing inside us.

Sky in the third eye

When we meditate on the *third eye*[3], we shall imagine the sky and our own Infinity. Our own Infinity's self-expansion we shall observe.

Sun in the crown centre

Then we shall meditate on the crown centre and imagine the sun, which is our own Immortality's new creation.

CONCENTRATION, MEDITATION AND CONTEMPLATION ON THE THIRD EYE

Concentration

Let us concentrate on the *third eye*, located in between the eyebrows and a little above. While concentrating, let us imagine for a few minutes just at the *third eye* a flame, a burning golden flame. What we call imagination is nothing short of an existence-reality, a world of its own. So let us concentrate, and while concentrating let us feel burning flames at our *third eye*.

Please breathe in as slowly as possible, as quietly as possible, and while breathing in try to feel that you are not breathing in through your nose; you are breathing in through your forehead. While breathing out you are also breathing through your forehead. Then please feel the presence of burning flames inside your forehead, precisely inside the *third eye*.

Meditation

Now let us meditate on the *third eye*. This time also, please breathe in and out through your forehead, and now imagine the planet sun or the inner sun, which is infinitely brighter than the planet sun. Please imagine at least one sun inside your forehead at the *third eye*, and inside that sun please imagine countless flames or rays of light. This time please keep your eyes fully open so that you can feel the vastness of the sun along with its light and power.

Contemplation

Now we shall contemplate. From the spiritual point of view, contemplation is the sweetest form of insep-arable oneness. This oneness is the oneness of the divine lover with the Beloved Supreme. The oneness that abides between the divine lover and the Beloved Supreme is called contemplation. It is by virtue of contemplation, proper contemplation, that we come to realise that we are not only divine seekers but also divine lovers, and that God is our Beloved Supreme.

We are like tiny drops, while God is the ocean. Countless drops form the ocean, and again, the ocean embodies the drops. First we imagined flames, then the sun itself.

When we can contemplate properly, we will become one with God Himself. When the seekers and God-lovers and God together play, sing and dance, at that time God is singing the song of multiplicity in unity. When the One Absolute remains in His transcendental aspect, and the seekers and God-lovers approach Him, then God is singing the song of unity in multiplicity.

So let us contemplate on the *third eye*. For a few minutes let us feel that we are the lover-flames; then we shall feel that we are the Beloved-Sun. Thus we shall change our respective roles.

Concentration-power, meditation-peace and contemplation-bliss

101

If I want to acquire power, then I shall concentrate on a very tiny reality. I shall focus all my attention on a little flame, and I shall, without fail, acquire concentration-power.

If I want to have peace, then I shall meditate on a very large reality. I shall meditate on the vast sky, and the vastness of the sky will inundate my inner being with peace.

And if I want to have bliss, then I shall contemplate on the sweetest, dearest and most intimate Oneness-Reality here on earth and there in Heaven—my Beloved Supreme.

Sweetness, fondness and oneness for contemplation

102

If you want to learn the art of contemplation, you need three important qualities: sweetness, fondness and oneness. Sweetness-capacity, fondness-capacity and oneness-capacity you have to develop.

In order to achieve the quality of sweetness, try to visualise right in front of you a lovely child—a beautiful, more beautiful, most beautiful child—and feel that all the qualities of the child are entering into you.

For the quality of fondness, you have to imagine the fondness of a mother for her child, or of a child for its mother. If you can achieve the fondness-capacity of a mother or a child, then you can rest assured that your heart has made tremendous progress.

To develop oneness, you have to visualise or imagine Heaven and earth at the same time. Try to recollect the Saviour Christ's supremely powerful oneness-message: "I and my Father are one." Here the Heavenly Father and the earthly son are inseparably one, and their oneness is nothing short of perfection and satisfaction. So, sweetness, fondness and oneness are the three supreme qualities an advanced seeker must develop in order to contemplate.

Concentration, meditation, contemplation and mantras

103 Put your hand between your eyebrows and a little above. Now say, "I am now concentrating. I know that my Lord Beloved Supreme is right above my head."

Put your right hand over your heart with the thumb on your heart. Now say, "I am now meditating. I can feel the blessingful Presence of my Lord Beloved Supreme right inside my heart."

Put your right hand over your heart and your left hand on your head. Please press both your head and your chest a little hard. As quietly and slowly as possible, you will breathe in and out. Now say, "I am now contemplating. I can vividly see my Lord Beloved Supreme right in front of my vision-eye, and He is telling me that He is eager to play with me the hide-and-seek game."

Put both hands right behind your head. Say, "My God-disappointment-past."

Now put the fingers of your right hand on your forehead, in between your eyebrows. Say, "My today's silver dreams."

Put your right hand on your heart and form a small circle. While forming a circle, feel you are forming the circle with light. Say, "My tomorrow's golden realities."

Simplicity, sincerity, purity and surety

There are quite a few meditation exercises a beginner can try. For the seeker wishing to enter the spiritual life, simplicity, sincerity, purity and surety are of utmost importance. It is simplicity that grants you peace of mind. It is sincerity that makes you feel that you are of God and that God is constantly for you. It is your pure heart that makes you feel at every moment that God is growing, glowing and fulfilling Himself inside you. It is surety that makes you feel that meditation is absolutely the right thing.

In silence kindly repeat the word "simplicity" inside your mind seven times and concentrate on the crown of your head. Then repeat the word "sincerity" seven times silently and soulfully inside your heart, and concentrate on your heart. Then kindly repeat the word "purity" seven times inside or around your navel centre, and concentrate on the navel centre[11]. Please do all this silently and most soulfully. Then focus your attention on the *third eye*, which is between and slightly above the eyebrows, and silently repeat "surety" seven times. Next, place your hand on top of your head and say three times, "I am simple, I am simple, I am simple." Then place your hand on your heart and say three times, "I am sincere, I am sincere, I am sincere." Then place your hand on the navel centre, repeating "I am pure," and on the *third eye*, repeating "I am sure."

SIMPLICITY, SINCERITY, HUMILITY, PURITY AND DIVINITY

Sri Chinmoy gave a flower to each person present during a meditation and then asked participants to meditate on the flower as he offered the following instruction:

The flower signifies beauty. Beauty is simplicity. Beauty is sincerity. Beauty is humility. Beauty is purity. Beauty is divinity.

Simplicity

Simplicity is the soul, and the soul is the direct representative of God. Now for a few minutes let us feel that we do not have a body, a vital[9], a mind or even a heart. Please try to feel that you have become the soul. Do not give any form to this idea. Just repeat in silence, 'soul, soul, soul', and feel that you have become a conscious and direct representative of God.

Sincerity

In the outer world, telling the truth is the highest form of sincerity. In the inner world, sincerity is seeing the Truth through God's Eye. Now let us feel that we have grown into inner sincerity and that we are seeing everything through God's Vision. Let us become inner sincerity.

106

Humility

In the inner world, humility always reminds us of what we were previously, of what we are now and of what we are going to become. It was by virtue of our humility that we accepted the spiritual life.

It is humility that cultivates within us the eagerness to know and to grow into higher realities. Everything is within us. But just because we are humble, the higher realities get the opportunity to fulfil themselves through us. Let us meditate on our sincere inner humility for a few minutes.

107

Purity

Physical purity is cleanliness, vital purity is an open heart and mental purity is the absence of undivine and unhealthy thoughts. Inner purity is our gratitude-heart. It is through gratitude, constant

108

gratitude to the Supreme in us, that we expand our consciousness and come to know our higher vision and reality. If we can sow a seed of gratitude which will germinate and grow into a tiny plant and then into a banyan tree, then under this huge banyan tree in our gratitude-hearts thousands of seekers will be able to take shelter and grow into divinity. For a few minutes let us feel that what we are and eternally will become is nothing but a gratitude-heart.

Divinity

Finally, the flower signifies divinity. The spiritual life is the life of the soul. We have to become consciously one with our soul. Why? Because it is only when we feel our oneness with the soul that true satisfaction can dawn in our lives. Now let us meditate on divinity, our own highest inner divinity.

Developing good qualities

There are many good things and many undivine, unaspiring things in our nature. We try to increase and multiply our good qualities and, at the same time, on the strength of our prayers and meditations, we try to decrease and eventually eliminate our undivine qualities.

Good qualities are like the fragrance of a flower. The flower is offering its fragrance, which embodies kindness, goodness, compassion and aspiration. If we cry inwardly for spiritual things — for Peace, Light, Bliss — then we are bound to achieve these divine qualities.

To develop beauty
I meditate inside a moonlit cave.
To develop humility
I meditate inside a tiny cave.
To develop purity
I meditate inside a sun-bathed cave.
To develop power
I meditate inside a spacious cave.

Compassion

A tree bending down

To develop compassion, meditate on a tree. Although the flowers, leaves and branches are above the ground, they are not looking downward with contempt or a feeling of superiority. The trunk of the tree may be very tall; the flowers, fruits and leaves may all be above us. But when we pass below the tree, the leaves, flowers and fruits say, "Take us; we are ready to be utilised by you." Because of its oneness with us, everything that the tree has, it is begging us to take.

110

Courage

The dynamic vital

If you want to conquer fear in the vital[9], try to expand the real vital in yourself. We use the aggressive vital, with its fighting quality, daily. But the dynamic vital, which is the real vital, wants to create something sooner than at once in a divine way, in an illumined way. So if we can concentrate on the dynamic vital and expand our consciousness there, then there can be no fear in the vital.

111

Digging deep within

If we want to conquer fear in the unaspiring heart, we have to take help directly from the soul. How many of us have seen the soul or felt it? When you meditate on the heart centre, try to feel, every time you breathe in, that you are digging inside.

This is not violent digging. No! It is only a divinely intensified feeling inside your heart that you are going deep, deep, deep within. Each time you breathe in, feel that you are going deeper within. And then, a few days or a few months later, you are bound to feel a tingle; you will hear a very tiny sound. When you hear the sound, try to see if the sound is caused by something or not. Normally when we hear a sound, it is because two hands are clapped together or two objects are struck together. But this sound in the soul is not the result of anything. It is spontaneous. When you feel that sound inside, like a celestial gong, then you are bound to conquer fear in your aspiring heart.

How to conquer fear?
With oneness within
And oneness without.
In oneness-light
There can be no fear.

Dynamism

Fire blazing all around

To increase your dynamism, meditate on flames. You can look at a candle flame or any other type of flame. Flames embody dynamism. Fire will burn all our lethargy or lack of enthusiasm. If fire burns our lethargy, then automatically dynamism will come to the fore. Just imagine that fire is blazing all around you. Immediately you will get up, you will run, you will do the needful with utmost speed.

Fire has dynamism. So always imagine flames or fire. If you imagine fire, you may think more of destruction than dynamism, but if you think of flames, climbing flames, then destruction will not come into your mind. Flames take us upward. How can we go upward without becoming dynamic? If I want to climb a tree, if I want to climb a mountain, then I have to be dynamic. Flames show us the way. They are going up, up, up and touching the sky. So, to increase your dynamism, look at flames.

Enthusiasm

Climb up for the mangoes

114

To have enthusiasm, feel that you are at the foot of a tree. When you look at the tree, you see that the most delicious mangoes, the ripest mangoes, are at the top, so naturally you will start climbing up with enthusiasm. But if you do not see the tree, and if you do not look up and see the flowers and fruits, then you will not have any enthusiasm to climb up.

Gratitude

The sweetness of a smile

115

Gratitude comes from sweetness. A child may not say "Thank you" to his mother, but the sweetness of his entire being is expressed through his eyes in the form of a smile. He does not know the word 'gratitude', but when the mother sees his sweet smile, she knows that the child is full of gratitude. So the more we can create sweetness in our hearts and in our being, the easier it becomes to offer gratitude to God.

One way to get sweetness is to look at a most beautiful, fragrant flower. When we look at the flower and smell its fragrance, consciously or unconsciously we become one with its beauty and fragrance. At that time, its sweetness enters into us or our own sweetness comes forward; sometimes both happen simultaneously.

If we are really focusing all our attention on the innocent beauty and fragrance of God the Creation through this flower, then jealousy and meanness disappear, and only sweet thoughts remain. And when sweetness comes to the fore in our nature, it becomes very easy to offer gratitude.

Expand into an elephant

To offer gratitude, try to feel that your gratitude is tinier than the tiniest, like an ant. But you will try to increase that gratitude into a huge elephant. You have to try to grow and expand it. When your gratitude is very huge, vast and strong, inside that powerful elephant try to have all the divine qualities: simplicity, sincerity, purity, humility and so forth. Feel that you have all these qualities inside your gratitude-heart.

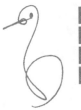

Decrease the number
Of your complaints.
Increase the power
Of your gratitude.

Humility

Grass or a tree

You can concentrate on a blade of grass or a small plot of green grass—anything that you feel is humble. Or you can look at a tree. How humble a tree is! In spite of having countless flowers, fruits and leaves, a tree is always self-giving and serves with such compassionate humility.

When the tree develops flowers and fruit, at that time the tree does not go up and touch the skies. It does not say, "I will have nothing to do with earth; earth is so bad, so ungrateful." Instead, the tree bends very nicely and shares its fruits with the world. Before the tree bears any fruit, the tree is for itself. But when it possesses something, when it starts bearing fruit, at that time it becomes for the world. The tree does not keep the fruits only for itself. The tree offers them for all the world to eat.

Inspiration

The garden of your heart

Your mind has to surrender to your heart. At every moment the heart is seeing a beautiful flower, whereas the mind is seeing a dry, dead tree. When you use the mind, you see a dead tree right in front of you, but when you use the heart, you see a most beautiful garden. Every time you meditate, imagine a garden with beautiful flowers. First imagine it right in front of you, and then try to imagine it inside your heart. In that way, the beauty and fragrance of the garden are bound to inspire you and make you feel that you are receiving something most precious.

The waves of the ocean

When you look at the ocean, you see huge waves. If you are using your heart to look at it, even with your ordinary naked eyes you will see that it is ever-new. But if you are using the mind, you will say, "Oh, it is the same thing, the same kind of waves." Nothing is boring if we have the right attitude.

A plane taking off

When you enter into any new field of activity, there is enthusiasm. Then afterwards it becomes monotonous, boring, and frustration starts. Now, think of a plane. When the plane takes off, it makes so much noise. It gives us the feeling that it will absolutely destroy everything around it. Once the plane is high in the air, its speed is much faster than when it was taking

off, but we hear practically no noise. And if the plane has a good pilot, will he not reach the destination? We have to keep in mind that the same Pilot who gave us the inspiration to hurry up and come to the airport, who put us into the plane, who made so much noise when the plane was taking off, is still piloting us to our Destination.

New ideas, new adventure

To overcome boredom in your meditation, use your imagination-power. Write down three absolutely new things that you have never done, you have never thought of. Then those three things will give you inspiration or a kind of challenge. They will create a sensation in your mind or in your being to do them. Life is not boring to one who believes in adventure. Adventure does not mean that you have to climb up the tallest mountain. To allow new ideas, fresh ideas, healthy ideas to enter into your mind—that is adventure.

You are an infant

Every day feel that you have taken new birth. If you feel that you are an infant, only a few hours old, then you are bound to feel that there is somebody who will take care of you. The mind always says that we have to take care of ourselves. But the heart says, "No, my father is there, my mother is there. They have infinite affection, infinite compassion, infinite fondness for me. They will take care of me." This is so true. God is both our Father and our Mother. God is only for those who feel that they are true children.

Intensity

Repeat 'intensity'

There are two ways we can increase our intensity. The first approach is to feel that all your strength, all your determination and will-power, is in one particular place, here inside your heart. Feel that you do not exist at all except in this tiny place. You do not have eyes, you do not have a nose, you do not have anything. Intensity will come only when you feel that your entire existence is concentrated at one particular place and not scattered.

The second way is to enter into your highest meditation. When you reach your absolutely highest meditation, just for two or three seconds utter the word 'intensity' with utmost will-power. When you utter the word 'intensity', like a bullet, intensity will enter into you. Not only will it enter into you, but it will also go out of you. Then this intensity will act like a miracle in your life.

Joy

124

Imagine a child

You can have the most joy just by imagining a child infinitely more beautiful than any child that you have seen in this world. You have inside you a child who is infinitely more beautiful. Just imagine it. While imagining you will get utmost joy.

Light

125

You are light

You want to know how you can receive light or how you can bring light to the fore. When you start your meditation or concentration, try to feel that you have come from light and you are inside light. This is not your imagination; this is not your mental hallucination. Far from it! When you start meditating, just feel what you are. It is a real, solid, concrete truth that you embody light and that you are light itself. You will see that there is a spontaneous flow of light from within. First you will feel it inside your heart; then you will feel it in your forehead, in the *third eye*; and finally you will feel it all over.

The purifying, energising breath

There is another way of seeing light. While breathing, when you draw in the breath, please feel that you are breathing in something that is purifying all that has to be purified inside you and, at the same time, energising all that is unfed. In the beginning, there are quite a few things inside you that have to be purified. There are quite a few things which are hungry. So when you feel that you are feeding, energising and at the same time purifying them, then you will see that light becomes absolutely natural.

Love

Breathe in a stream of love

When you are breathing in, feel a stream of divine love flowing in and through your body. You love yourself, you love God, you love your dearest and nearest ones, and you love humanity as a whole. So first please try to bring to the fore God's love aspect. Love is the pioneer of all divine qualities. So when you cry for God, feel love—immediate, spontaneous, unreserved, soulful love.

Repeat 'love' throughout your body

128

Every day when you meditate, please say the word 'love' before you start your meditation. When you utter the word 'love', try to feel that your arms, your legs, your eyes and every part of you has increased its capacity. When you say the word 'love', you have to feel that your arms have become stronger, not to strike anybody, but to work for humanity. Then concentrate on your eyes and try to feel that you are using your eyes to see only good things in everybody. When you concentrate on your ears, feel that you want to hear only good things, encouraging and inspiring things. Each time you say the word 'love', concentrate on one of your organs. Then afterwards, try to concentrate on your inner consciousness. Try to expand it.

Become the fragrant flower

129

Feel that you have entered into a garden with many, many flowers. Choose one flower that you like and go near it. Appreciate its beauty and smell its fragrance. Then just say a few times, "How I wish I could be as pure and as beautiful as this flower." After five minutes, try to imagine that an infinitesimal amount of beauty from that flower has entered into you. Then gradually try to feel that all the good qualities you are seeing in the flower—its beauty, its purity, its fragrance and so on—have entered into you and are inside you.

Now remember how much you loved that flower and how much joy it gave you. At first it had a separate existence. But little by little you brought its beauty and reality inside your own body and inside your own heart. Then try to feel that you do not have a body, you do not have a mind, you do not have anything. Think of yourself only as that most beautiful flower. Because you have become that beautiful flower, you are bound to appreciate yourself and love yourself the way that you loved the flower.

Feel God loves you more

130

Once you start loving yourself, you have to feel that God loves you infinitely more. If you are suffering from a physical ailment or something else, you may feel that nobody is there to love you or sympathise with you. But there is Someone and that Person is inside you—if you are suffering, then you have to know that He is suffering infinitely more. If you are happy, then He is infinitely happier.

Try to cultivate the feeling that the Supreme, who is your highest part, is always feeling what you are feeling, only infinitely more. So if you love yourself, then He loves you infinitely more.

Newness

The rising sun

131

Every morning meditate on the sun. Although it is the same sun that is rising, every day we can see a new beauty inside the sun. Our mind is telling us that it is the same sun that we saw yesterday and the day before yesterday. But when the heart sees this same sun, there is tremendous joy, tremendous thrill, tremendous ecstasy.

We have to see and feel everything with the heart, not with the mind. The mind will tell us, "I have seen the sun already; I have been seeing it for so many years. There is nothing new in it." But when the heart sees the same sun, the heart sees something new, with a thrilling sensation. That thrilling sensation itself is creating something new, and that newness is creating something special.

For the heart, every day is new, like the sun. When the sun rises, the mind will not care to look at the sun because the mind feels that it is the same old thing. Whether the sun is coming out of the water or out of the clouds, the mind does not care.

But the heart is waiting for the sun. The heart says, "When will it come? When will it come? When will it come?" The heart's eagerness always sees newness in everything. If we use the heart, then everything is new. Every day, even though we are doing and seeing the same thing outwardly, the heart is constantly feeling new joy, new joy, new joy.

A child entering a garden

Feel that you are a child entering into a garden. When a grown-up enters into a garden every day, he sees the flowers and says, "They are all the same as they were yesterday." A child of four or five sees the same flowers that the grown-up sees, but he gets a totally different kind of experience, which is all joy. When his heart sees a flower, that flower is something new for him. We see the same kinds of flowers for so many days, and once we see them, it is enough for us. Even the second day, it is all old. But every time the child sees the garden, for him everything is new.

You are seven years old

If you can feel sincerely that you are a seven-year-old girl or boy, so much poison that is inside your mind will disappear and easily you will be able to escape from your mind-jungle. Such enthusiasm and joy will enter into your life! Every day you will see your life in a new way and your sweet, sweeter, sweetest qualities you will be able to bring forward once again. At that time, you will blossom like a flower, petal by petal. For a seven-year-old child there is no doubt, no depression, no frustration, no negativity. The child is just jumping with joy and playing and playing in his heart-garden.

Patience

Goal in the distance

134

Feel that you are seeing a garden two miles away. You have to tell yourself, "No matter how difficult the road is, if only I can arrive there, I will get so much joy. As soon as I reach the flowers and breathe in their fragrance, I will be the happiest person." If you keep in mind the goal of happiness, then automatically you will develop patience.

Peace

Heart chakra and crown chakra

135

There are two chakras one can invoke for peace. One is the heart chakra[1] and the other is the crown chakra[7]. If we go to the heart centre, the peace that we will get will be only for our earthly existence, our daily activities. In the case of the heart, we will not be affected if the people around us are quarrelling or fighting. But if we go beyond this chakra and open up the crown centre, the *Sahasrara* chakra or thousand-petaled lotus, we will get infinite Peace, eternal Peace and transcendental Peace, because that chakra is connected with the highest height.

Slowly or quickly

If you feel nervous or upset, there are two ways to bring down peace. One way is to breathe in quietly and say 'Supreme'[2] three times very slowly. But if you find this difficult, you can invoke the Supreme as fast as possible. Fear or anxiety has a speed of its own. If you are about to be attacked by your enemy, then try to utter the Name of the Supreme much faster than the speed of the attack you are getting from anger or fear. If you can do this, the Supreme will immediately conquer your anger, frustration or fear.

Invoke the colour blue

Among the colours, blue is the best in order to invoke peace, because blue indicates Infinity. When one has Infinity, then he automatically invokes peace. Each colour has peace, but one can invoke peace best with blue.

Perfection

Remain one-pointed

138

To attain perfection, our meditation has to be one-pointed. It cannot be the kind of meditation in which the mind is one-pointed one moment and the next moment it is roaming in a wild forest—thinking of our friends or what we had for breakfast. If a single thought enters through the mind's door, it is like a nail being hammered into the wall of our meditation. If there are no thoughts, then there is no hammer, no nail, nothing—just peace. Unfortunately, this kind of meditation is extremely difficult to have.

Progress

Pilgrimage to the sun

139

To make faster progress, think of the sun and think of yourself as a pilgrim who is either running or flying towards the sun. Or you can imagine a sun inside you that is extremely, extremely beautiful—infinitely more beautiful and more powerful than the outer sun. Feel that as a pilgrim, you are running as fast as possible, and the faster you are running, the more beauty, the more power, the more light, the more affection, the more love, the more fondness you are seeing in the inner sun. The faster you are running towards the sun, the more its own divine qualities are increasing, and at the same time they are beckoning you. The inner sun has all these divine qualities: love, affection, sweetness, fondness, concern and so on. If you can see yourself as a pilgrim running towards the sun, you will be able to make the fastest progress.

The sun dispelling the clouds

140

When you look at the morning sun, darkness disappears. At first the sun may be covered by clouds, but then it emerges from the clouds. Similarly, our human nature—our whole existence—has to come out of darkness. Then only can we make the fastest progress.

Again, you have to make progress slowly and steadily, not overnight. God-realisation is not like instant coffee.

Purity

Where to find purity

141

The best place to meditate for purity is the heart. Meditate on the heart, and the moment you feel the presence of light there, bring it into your navel. Then try to imagine that the navel centre[11], the vital, is constantly circling or that there is a disk that is rotating all around it. It is going on, going on. And while it is turning, you just repeat, "Supreme, Purity, Supreme, Purity." Or you can say, "Purity is the Supreme, the Supreme is Purity." That is even easier.

Concentrate on a flower

142

As soon as you look at a flower, your mind becomes beautiful, your mind becomes pure, your mind becomes fragrant. If you look at a flower, your mind will be filled with pure thoughts. But you have to look at the flower most sincerely and intensely. You cannot gaze at it casually and allow your mind to roam freely. Your power of concentration has to be on the flower.

Look at a flower early in the morning and smell its fragrance, and immediately you will feel how pure the flower is. Or you can feel that there is a flower inside your heart blossoming petal by petal, let us say a rose or a lotus. The moment you see a flower, consciously or unconsciously you breathe in the purity of that flower. If you feel that a rose is blossoming petal by petal from within, then naturally the fragrance and purity of the rose will permeate your whole inner and outer existence.

Become a candle flame

If you do not have a flower, you can also use a candle flame. Do not concentrate on the base or the wax, but only on the flame. Imagine that you have become the flame itself. By looking at the flame, you will see that it is burning away all your impurities. The candle flame is constantly climbing up high, higher, highest. While it is climbing, it is illumining your ignorant existence.

Become the vast sky

One way to develop purity is to observe a small object, such as a flower or a flame. Again, by observing something larger than the largest, you can also develop purity. Look at the sky. That is the first step. The next step is to feel that you are inside the sky. First look at it, how vast it is. Then look at one portion of the sky and imagine that you have entered into it. Once you have entered into it, try to become the vastness itself. Impurity comes from the limited mind, whereas purity comes from vastness. The human mind is impure because the human mind is unable to become one with the Universal Reality. If something is vaster than the vastest—the sky or the sun or the Himalayas—then that vastness itself can give you purity.

In the depths of the ocean

Another way to develop purity is to imagine the ocean. On the surface you are seeing that the ocean is full of turmoil and restlessness, but at the bottom there is poise. You can imagine that you are entering into the depths of the ocean.

These are several ways you can try. You can look at a flower or a flame. Again, you can choose something that is vaster than the vastest, higher than the highest or deeper than the deepest. Imagine that thing and try to enter into it.

Your mind full of fragrance

Purity is already inside your heart—inside everybody's heart. The mind is the part of us that lacks purity. So you have to exercise your imagination. Imagine that your mind is a most beautiful flower—whatever flower you like most, which gives you utmost joy. Imagine that you do not have a nose, or ears, or eyes; only feel that your entire head is a most beautiful flower that is full of fragrance.

Then look at your flower-face in the mirror. While looking lovingly at the flower for a few seconds, you cannot have undivine thoughts. When the beauty and fragrance of the flower are entering into your mind, you cannot think of undivine things.

Image in a mirror

147

Look at yourself in the mirror and feel that you are totally one with the physical being that you are seeing. Then try to enter into the image that you are seeing. From there you should try to grow. You will grow with one thought: God wants you and you need God. Repeat: "God wants me, I need God. God wants me, I need God." Then you will see that slowly, steadily and gradually this divine thought is entering into you and permeating your inner and outer existence, giving you purity in your mind, vital and body.

Breathe in purity, breathe out impurity

148

Quietly and slowly breathe in and feel that with each breath you are bringing into your system peace, light and bliss. These qualities are nothing but purity itself. Then, when you breathe out, feel that you are breathing out all the ignorance and imperfection inside you. Through conscious breathing you can bring purity into your system; and each time you breathe out, throw out impurity.

Purity you want?
Just imagine breathing in the beauty,
Purity and fragrance of a flower.

Breathe in through your heart, out through your crown chakra

149

Impurity does not originate inside you; it is coming from outside—from the undivine consciousness of the outer world. It starts with the breath, when you inhale. Our impurity does not start below the navel; it starts in the nose, when we breathe in, and then it goes downward. So when you breathe in, you have to feel that it is the flower that is breathing in; you have to feel that the beauty and fragrance of the flower are receiving everything that is coming inside you.

Early in the morning breathe in consciously seven times, and while you breathe in try to feel that you are actually breathing in through your heart and not through your nose. Try to feel that your breath is entering you through your heart centre[1]. And while you are breathing out try to feel that your breath is going up, up to the top of your head and out through the thousand-petalled lotus, the crown centre[7] at the top of your head. If you can feel, and not just imagine, that you are breathing through your heart, immediately purity will enter and start revolving and functioning in you. When purity starts performing its role, impurity from the navel and lower centres travels up and is released. Do this early in the morning and in the evening also, if possible. Then your system is bound to be purified.

The sun and the moon

Look at the morning sun, the early rising sun. How beautiful it is! Do you see anything impure in it? No. Look at the moon. Do you see anything impure? Anything that you feel is outwardly pure, keep that thing right in front of your mental vision when you meditate.

Enter the seven higher worlds

While breathing in, with each breath try to repeat 'Supreme' slowly seven times, and again do it seven times while breathing out. Inside you there are seven higher worlds and seven lower worlds. When you repeat 'Supreme' while breathing in, feel that you are going into the seven higher worlds inside you. Once you have reached the seven higher worlds, you will find solid power.

When you breathe out, think of the seven lower worlds within you and try to throw the strength of the higher worlds into them. Accumulate everything in the higher worlds and then, when you are breathing out and saying 'Supreme, Supreme, Supreme...', enter into the lower worlds with peace, light and bliss to purify the lower worlds. First go up; then enter into the lower worlds where it is all ignorance and impurity. If you can purify the lower worlds after having reached the heights, you do not have to worry at all.

Receptivity

Repeat 'Supreme' in your crown chakra

152   There are many ways to develop receptivity or to get immediate receptivity. Two ways I can tell you. One way is to repeat the word 'Supreme' over and over again, as fast as possible—just as fast as the Indian musicians say *'Sa, re, ga, ma, pa, da, ni, sa.'* But it must be done in silence. First select one place in your body, let us say your crown centre[7] *[at the top of the head]*, and concentrate there while repeating 'Supreme' as fast as possible. Then select another spot and concentrate there, and repeat 'Supreme' again. It is better to go from the top down than from the bottom up.

It does not have to be a psychic centre. It can be any place that you like. Suppose you like your right eye. Then concentrate there and chant 'Supreme, Supreme, Supreme' in silence.

Or if I have given you a spiritual name, you can chant your own name, or 'Guru, Guru, Guru[4]', or any other thing in which you have all faith. Since you always have faith in the Supreme, that is usually the best.

If you can do this in seven different places in your body, at one particular place you are bound to find yourself receptive. You can concentrate anywhere—

the head, the forehead, the heart, the navel, the foot—anywhere. In at least one particular place, if you have concentrated seriously, you are bound to receive. Receptivity does not always have to be in the heart. Even in the foot you can receive something.

Bring light into your heart

153

Receptivity is the flow of cosmic energy and cosmic light. When you concentrate on any place, try to bring light into yourself. After you have brought it inside, the next thing is to bring it to the absolutely right place, the heart. The best reservoir to store what you have received is the heart.

The child lost in the woods

154

Another way to create receptivity is to make yourself feel that you are only three years old, a mere babe in the woods. You have no mother, no father, no brother, no sister, nobody at all to protect you, and you are alone in a forest on a very, very dark night. All around you is darkness.

Nobody is there to help you; death is dancing right in front of you, and you are totally lost. Then what do you do? You cry within for help: "Save me! Save me! I have nobody here! Save me!" When that kind of inner cry comes, the Supreme is bound to open your heart, or I will be there to say, "Do not feel helpless; you are God's child. Why should you have to be insecure?"

At times you are not receptive just because you have become too secure; you have become complacent because you are satisfied with your material possessions. Once you are satisfied with the things that you have, why should you cry for something more? When you have this kind of complacent feeling, at that time your inner cry ceases.

But if you feel that you are absolutely helpless, and that you are desperately in need of God, then naturally your inner cry will be strong. You need not feel that you are helpless and lost every day and every hour— far from it. But if you are complacent, if you feel that what you have is sufficient, then why should God take care of you? You do not need His Help. As long as you are complacent, you can have no receptivity. You have to change your attitude; you have to feel that you are totally, totally helpless and lost without God.

Offer your gratitude

155

The easiest and most effective way to increase your receptivity is to offer your deepest gratitude to the Supreme, each day before you meditate. When an individual offers gratitude to God, immediately his receptivity increases. His vessel becomes large. Then God is able to pour more of His Blessings into the person or enter more fully into that vessel with His own divine Existence. God is infinite, but only according to our receptivity can He enter into us. God is like sunlight. If I leave this window open, sunlight will come in here. If I keep all the other windows closed, it cannot come in there. The more we offer gratitude, the more we increase our receptivity and capacity. The more windows we open, the more God enters into us with Light, abundant Light, infinite Light. When we offer gratitude, immediately God's Light comes pouring into our being.

When you pray,
Think of a lost child within you
Crying helplessly.
When you meditate,
Think of a morning flower
Smiling and smiling,
Radiating its beauty
And offering its fragrance.
This is how you can make friends
With your soul
And fly with it infinitely higher
Than the confines of the mind.

Make a pond into a sea

If you see that you have a little receptivity, then dig more. Do not be satisfied with the receptivity that you have. Today, if it is a tiny pool, make it into a pond, then make it into a big lake, then into a sea. Receptivity can be expanded like that, gradually. Starting with a small hole, gradually make it large, larger, largest. Once you receive some light, try to grow into the light itself.

Increase your physical strength

Some people need to be physically stronger in order to receive more. Otherwise, you will not be able to develop more receptivity. When light, abundant light, descends from Above, it will be very difficult for you to hold it if you are not physically stronger.

Two flowers

While you are placing a flower on your shrine, try to feel that this flower is reminding you of your heart, which you want to be as beautiful as the flower. You cannot see your heart, but you can look at a flower and say, "How I wish my heart were as beautiful as this flower!"

Then try to feel that this flower is breathing, the same way that your heart is taking in your life-breath. Connect your heart-flower and the outer flower. While you are looking at the flower on the shrine, feel that your breath is entering into it. Then again, feel that the flower has entered into your heart and there it is breathing. Your heart-flower and the flower that you have placed on the shrine are going to and fro; they are constantly interchanging. The flower that is on the shrine is entering into your heart, and again it is coming out to be on the shrine.

If you can do this during your meditation, then your heart will become purer than the purest, and you will be able to absorb God's Compassion, Love, Blessings—anything that He wants to give you—in absolutely abundant measure because your heart is all ready to receive.

Inner joy

159

Another way to expand your receptivity during your meditation is to try to consciously feel inner joy. If you cannot feel inner joy immediately, then try to imagine for a few seconds or a few minutes that you have it. This will not be false. Your imagination will intensify your aspiration and help you to bring forward true inner joy in the course of time. The very nature of inner joy is expansion. When you expand, your receptivity will automatically increase, like a vessel that keeps getting larger.

Simplicity

Speak like a child

160

To simplify your life, just think of yourself as a four-year-old child. Try to imagine the way he thinks of reality. If you have to form a sentence, instead of twenty words, just use three or four words. If you have to talk to someone about a so-called complicated matter, see how you can simplify it. No matter with whom you are talking, you have to feel that you are a child and that person is also a child. Always try to have a childlike consciousness and to see each and every human being as another child. When a childlike quality comes into your life, everything automatically becomes simple.

Sincerity

Cry like a baby

161

Try to imagine right in front of you a baby crying pitifully for its mother's attention. The cry of a baby is absolutely sincere. Try to identify with the sincere cry the child has. If you can identify yourself with the child's cry, with its helplessness, then sincerity will automatically dawn.

Surrender

The drop entering the ocean

162

First think of a tiny drop of water and then throw that tiny drop into the sea. When you do that, you will not be able to see the drop any longer. You will see the sea itself. You do not want to surrender or you find it difficult to surrender because you feel that if you do, then you will no longer exist. But what happens when the drop enters into the sea is that it becomes one with the sea. Think of yourself as a drop and think of God as the ocean. This moment you are a tiny drop— outside, alone and helpless—and the next moment you are one with the vast ocean.

Replace your existence with the Supreme

163

Stand about three and a half feet *[one metre]* away from a wall. Then, make a very tiny black circle on the wall at eye level, and inside the circle make one dot. It has to be black. With your eyes half open, gaze at the circle, focusing all your attention on it. Try not to see anything else except the circle. After two or three minutes, try to feel that you are totally one with the circle, that your whole existence is inside it. Then go beyond the circle to the other side of the wall. When you go through the circle and beyond it, try to look back at your own physical reality, the reality that is standing in front of the wall. You started from the physical body, but now you have sent your subtle body to the other side of the wall. From there try to look back at your physical. This will give you some satisfaction.

Complete satisfaction will come when you look at only the dot inside the circle, and not the circle itself. Try to see your own self there, your own face of aspiration. Feel that you exist only there and nowhere else. Then try to feel that your existence, your face, your consciousness, everything, is replaced by the Supreme. Once you feel that your previous existence has been totally replaced by the Supreme, you will have established your inseparable oneness with the Will of the Supreme.

Truth

The illumining flame

164 If you want to feel the clarity of Truth, please always try to see the burning, illumining flame within you which is constantly trying to illumine the unlit part of you.

Listen to the inner message

165

Go deep within and try to listen to the message of your inner being. Try to feel that there is Someone who is always ready at every moment to offer you a divine message. Inside this message you will see the clarity of Truth. Then it is up to you to utilise this clarity in your life of aspiration. There are many people on earth who have not heard the inner message. Again, there are many who have heard the inner message of Truth, yet they find it difficult to apply what they have learned in their day-to-day life because of their lack of faith in themselves. They see the Truth, but they feel that this Truth is so vast that it will devour them if they try to utilise it. This is absurd. Truth cannot devour or destroy anybody; it only energises, illumines and fulfils us.

Will-power

The sun blazing in the forehead

166

Let us meditate on our forehead. Let us imagine that it is now midday. It is twelve o'clock and the sun is very, very bright. It is a blazing sun inside our forehead, in between the eyebrows but slightly above. There burns a blazing sun and it is twelve o'clock noon. This is for our identification with the will-power consciousness.

Dig deep into your heart

167

The easiest and most effective way to cultivate will-power is to concentrate on your heart and then dig there every day. But do not be satisfied with your digging. Today you have dug and you have come to a certain point. Then tomorrow again you have to dig further. The deeper you can go, the sooner you will feel and see the light. First you feel, then you see, then you become. First you will feel that there is something inside like a very tiny insect: that is the light. Then you will see it with your inner vision or with your human vision. Finally you will grow into it.

Feel the pulse in your thumb

168

Hold the end of your thumb tightly with your first finger, and try to feel a pulsation only in the tip of your thumb. Feel that that pulsation is your life energy, your breath, your mission, your realisation, soul and Goal. It is all there in the tip of your thumb. Then look at your thumbnail and feel that there is your dream and reality. When an idea comes to you to do something, you will get all the will-power you need from your thumb.

Incidentally, the thumb can also be used to determine whether or not a person has will-power. If a person's thumb is pointed at the end, generally that person has will-power. The more pronounced the point, the more will-power he is likely to have.

Go deep into your third eye

Sit cross-legged in front of a very small mirror, with your back straight. Do not hold the mirror in your hand, but set it up at eye level, so that you will be able to see only your face. Try to see your *third eye*. Inside your *third eye* imagine a deep hole, and try to see inward, not downward, through the hole. Go as far in as possible. When you reach your ultimate capacity, try to see all your love there—the love that you have for your life. When you have seen all your love, try to imagine the Supreme in that place. Feel there is your love-field and offer it to the Supreme. Then you will be able to accomplish in the inner world all the things that you wanted to do.

Will-power in the body, vital, mind and heart

Physical will-power enables you to keep your body firm, but not stiff. You will not move to and fro during your meditation. Your physical will-power will keep you properly stationed in one place. To use your physical will-power, feel that divine energy is descending and flowing like a river all over the body.

Vital will-power is the outgoing energy or thought of dominating others. While you are meditating, you may have some desire to show your friends that you are far superior to them. Instead, expand yourself, feel that you are like a bird and you are spreading your wings to cover each and every one in the whole world.

Mental will-power is operating when you think you know much more than others. Instead, use your mind's will-power to eliminate any thought. The best use of your mental will-power is not to allow any thought to enter your mind.

If you use your psychic will-power, which is the heart's will, then you will feel that you have become inseparably one with the rest of the world. During meditation it is always safest to use your psychic will, heart's will, oneness.

Meditations for artists and musicians

Meditation can increase our creativity. Prayer and meditation are the only way. Many people are not born poets or born artists. But by practising meditation, they bring into their system literary capacities, painting capacities, musical capacities, because meditation means new life. When new life enters into you, you become a new man.

Since life itself is an art,
We must pray to God
To make us His choice artists.

For musicians

Meditate before performing

If we pray and meditate and then start playing music, naturally we shall express what we have received from our prayer and meditation. Before we play, if we can meditate for even two or three minutes and acquire an iota of peace or bliss, then this peace and bliss will definitely enter into our music, into our instrument, into our voice. Then our music will automatically become spiritual and divine.

171

Offer your life-breath to your instrument

While you are breathing in and breathing out, try to feel that you are offering your life-breath to the instrument keys that you will use. Your life-breath is something very precious, and you are offering your life's most precious thing to your instrument.

172

Softness in your voice

To bring forward the spiritual qualities of your voice, meditate on softness. A flower will give you softness, or you can meditate on anything that is very delicate. But do not think of anything sharp. A spontaneous flow comes from softness; it does not come from sharpness. If you can meditate on something that is very, very soft, it will make your voice sweeter.

Otherwise, you can meditate on your soul for a few seconds before you sing. But if you try mentally to bring forward your voice, even if you succeed, it will not last for more than a few seconds.

Soulful singing

To sing soulfully, try to visualise a beautiful garden inside your heart. If you see a beautiful garden, then soulfulness automatically will come. Or feel that you are seated alone at the foot of a tree, facing a river. That also will help you.

Overcoming nervousness

Take all the members of the audience as one person, and feel that this person is yourself. If you see many people watching you, naturally you become nervous. You feel that they are judging you or criticising you.

But if you take all of them as yourself, then you will not be nervous. When you are singing by yourself, even if you sing incorrectly, you do not become nervous because there is nobody to hear it. You are the singer, and you are also the audience. So when you are singing in public, take the whole audience as one individual, and then see that individual as none other than yourself. At that time, nervousness goes away.

For artists

You are the instrument

176

Before you start painting, just think of yourself as an instrument. You hold your brush and you know that it is your instrument. In the same way you can look at your hand, arms, wrist or fingers and repeat a few times, "This is not mine, this is Yours, O Supreme." Look at your fingers and say, "These fingers are not mine. These fingers are of the Supreme and for the Supreme. This wrist, this palm is not mine; it is the Supreme's for the Supreme." The paint, the canvas, you, anything that you are going to use, you have to look at individually and say, "This is not mine; it is the Supreme's. If it is His, then it is His responsibility."

See with the eye of your heart

While painting, you have to not use your mind at all. If you use your mind, all kinds of fear can enter. Even if the mind feels that your painting is beautiful, five minutes later the mind may say, "Oh, it is not beautiful." So never see anything with your mind's eye. See everything with your heart's eye. Then you will see that everything is beautiful.

Become one with the brush and the paint

If you use the heart, you become one with your painting and you will never be afraid of it. But also, you have to become one with the brush and the paint for they are the instruments that you are using. So become one with the painting and one with the instruments—the brush and the canvas. Then one instrument is becoming another instrument, and the real Doer is the Supreme. If you can do this, then there can be no fear, no doubt and no sense of failure.

See the seed-essence first

To see the inner beauty of something you want to paint or draw, first meditate for at least five minutes and try to see the essence of the thing you want to paint. Feel that there is a seed inside you, and then try to feel the seed germinating and growing into a plant. Then feel that this tiny plant is growing into a huge tree and this tree is your painting. First see the essence and then see the total substance. First make your creation as small as possible, then make it as vast as possible. Try to see the microcosm and the macrocosm together. Then try to see a bridge between the two, connecting the smallest and the largest, or try to connect them with your aspiration. As soon as you see the connection, you are bound to see the beauty from its origin to its culmination in your painting.

First see life in your creation, then see light in your creation. Or you can do it the other way. First you can see light in your creation, then you can see life in your creation. While you are imagining the seed, try to feel at that time that you are meditating on light; and when you are seeing the tree, feel that you are meditating on life. Or do it the other way. Whether you take the tree, the culmination, as life or light, or the seed within you as life or light, automatically you will bring forward beauty in your painting. That is because, before it has come into the physical world, in the inner world you have already given life and light to it. When you give life or light to something that you are going to create, you are bound to see beauty in it.

Paint something spiritual

180

To bring purity into your consciousness while you are painting, you have to paint spiritual things, and then you have to identify your consciousness with the divine qualities of these things. "Art for art's sake," from the spiritual point of view, is wrong. Suppose you have drawn a ballpoint pen. Everybody will say, "Yes, it is a wonderful ballpoint pen that he has drawn." But what inspiration or aspiration have you gained from this? None! The drawing has not elevated your consciousness even an inch. But if you draw a beautiful white flower, then immediately your eyes will appreciate the beauty and divinity of the flower. And even while you are drawing the flower, you are receiving purity from it.

Divinity is inside the pen and it is also inside the flower. But the divinity that is inside the flower is much more fulfilling and much more fully manifested. So when you draw a flower, your consciousness will be elevated. And when your consciousness is elevated, at that time purity has entered into you.

Suppose you draw a tree. A tree stands patiently and protects everybody from the rain and sun, and it offers its fruits to the whole world. The inner essence of a tree is patience and sacrifice. These qualities may not yet be manifested in you, but they have already been manifested in the tree. So when you draw a tree, try to enter into the divine qualities of the tree and identify with them. Then the divine qualities that it possesses will be yours.

If you draw a spiritual Master and enter into the consciousness of that Master, you will be flooded with inner purity. For two or three hours you will be drawing him and meditating on him, so naturally his consciousness will enter into you. After drawing spiritual Masters, Indian artists have achieved lifelong purity based on their inner identification with these Masters. This is what you can do, too.

Feel the consciousness of your subject

181

Whenever you draw something spiritual, try to feel the significance of what you are drawing. When you are drawing a river, if you see it flowing just as thousands of other rivers in the world are flowing, then it is useless. Water symbolizes consciousness. So you have to see the river as a flow of consciousness going to its source, the infinite ocean. You have to feel that the river is movement—not restless movement but dynamic movement. The river is the finite, and it is entering into the ocean, which is infinite. Similarly, while you are drawing you have to feel that you are also entering into the Source. Then, since you know that water represents consciousness, try to feel while drawing that consciousness is entering into you and that you are expanding your consciousness.

The significance of colours

182

Colours signify different things. The colour silver, for instance, has a special significance, which is applicable to every field. Silver means purity. When you see this colour during meditation, you have to know that you have achieved tremendous progress in your life in terms of purity. When you see the colour silver, at that time you have to feel that your mind is becoming pure, your vital[9] is becoming pure, your body-consciousness is becoming pure. This also applies when you see the colour silver in art.

The sincere seeker can concentrate and meditate on these colour plates *[in Sri Chinmoy's book Colour Kingdom, which gives the spiritual quality associated with many different colours]* in order to bring to the fore the qualities which the colours embody. The colour which will help you bring forward a quality, which you lack now, is the right colour for you to concentrate on. You yourself have to make the choice. The colour that gives you the greatest joy, or immediate joy, or the colour, which you feel you have an affinity for, is the one that naturally you will choose. If you put a few of the colours in front of you, and one of the colours pulls you like a magnet, then that is the colour for you—for your realisation and manifestation.

Meditations
for runners

Sport is a natural complement to meditation, and vice-versa. Meditation helps us to discover our hidden capacities and to access our unlimited inner potential. With the help of meditation an athlete can not only increase their physical performance, but also transform the joy derived from their sport into a permanent and deep satisfaction. Conversely, sport helps meditation by silencing the mind and purifying our whole being. It also teaches us how to constantly expand our own outer and inner capacities.

In your meditation
If you are desperately trying
To reach the acme of perfection
But you are failing,
Do not give up.
As one who does the long jump
Rests in between each attempt,
Wait and try again.
Who knows, in your next attempt
You may do extremely well.

KEEP UP YOUR ENTHUSIASM

In short distances—from 100 metres to a mile—it is easy to maintain enthusiasm. You get a burst of energy or inspiration and you go. But for long distances, to maintain enthusiasm is very difficult. There are many, many ways to keep your enthusiasm when you are getting tired in long distance, but here are two ways that are particularly effective.

Think of yourself as a child

While running, do not think of yourself as twenty-five or thirty years old. Only think of yourself as six or seven years old. At the age of six or seven, a child does not sit; he just runs here and there. So imagine the enthusiasm of a young child and identify yourself, not with the child, but with the source of his enthusiasm. This is one way.

Breathe with other runners

Another secret way, if you are running long distance, is to identify yourself with ten or even twenty runners who are ahead of you. Only imagine the way they are breathing in and breathing out. Then, while you are inhaling, feel that you are breathing in their own breath and that the energy of the twenty runners is entering into you. Then, while you are exhaling, feel that all twenty runners are breathing out your tiredness and lack of enthusiasm.

While you are running, it may be difficult for you to feel that cosmic energy is entering into you. So occultly or secretly you can try breathing in the breath of twenty runners at a time. The energy which you will receive, which is nothing but enthusiasm, will let you go ten steps forward. But you have to remember that you are breathing in their breath, their inspiration and determination, and not their tiredness. You have to feel that their breath is like pure, distilled water. If you think of someone who is not running well, that person's breath will not help you. But if you think of someone who is running faster than you, his energy will help you. You are not stealing it; only you are taking in the spiritual energy that is all around him and inside him, just as it is inside you. But because he is running faster, you are more conscious of it in him.

Increasing your speed

185

To a great extent, speed in running starts in the mind. Try to develop more imagination. Imagine that you are running fast, and appreciate your speed. Then let the thrill and joy that you get from your imagination inundate you. This joy in itself will increase your speed. You can also think of some people who really do run fast and try to identify yourself with them.

Mantra for running

While running, if you can repeat the name of the Supreme most soulfully and devotedly, then naturally it will help you improve your speed and endurance. If you want a mantra, then 'Supreme'[2] is the best mantra. If you want a special type of meditation, then 'Supreme' is the best type of meditation. Just try to repeat the name of the Supreme most soulfully. It will help you improve your speed and increase your power of endurance.

There are two ways to repeat God's name. Even if you are running a marathon, if you are inspired to repeat God's name as fast as possible, then do it; again, if you are inspired to draw deep breaths and very slowly and quietly repeat God's name, then that is also most effective.

Before you pray and meditate
You must invoke the deer-speed.

While you are praying and meditating,
You must invoke the elephant-confidence.

After you have prayed and meditated,
You must invoke the lion-victory.

Imagine a tiger chasing you

187

To increase your speed, try to feel that you are being chased rather than being pulled by something or someone. That way you will go faster. If somebody is chasing you, your speed will be faster than if somebody in front of you is pulling you towards him with a rope. If you feel that a magnet is pulling you to the finish line, you will run fast; but you will run faster if you feel that somebody is chasing you and you are running for your life. Imagine that a ferocious tiger is right behind you and at any moment is going to devour you. You know how fast a tiger can run! So you will run for your most precious life, and you will run the fastest. Or think that your house has caught fire and you are running to the nearest telephone booth to call the fire department.

If you cannot think of a tiger or a fire, then try to feel that you are one or two metres ahead of everyone else right from the beginning. Before the race has started even, when you are taking the set position at the starting blocks, please try to feel that the other five or six runners are behind you. Then, when you start, feel that they are not running with you but are chasing you because you are trying to eat something most delicious and they want to deprive you of it. If you can feel that your rivals are behind you, chasing you, then you will be able to run much faster than if you see that the others are all on a line with you. So if you can feel that your competitors are a little behind and chasing you, and that you are running for your life, this will give you more inner intensity and outer determination.

The dynamism and peace of the sea

188

To bring the power of your meditation into your running, always think that you are standing in front of the sea. The surface of the sea is very dynamic; it is all waves and surges. But the bottom of the sea is all calmness and peace. You can identify yourself with the surface of the sea and also with its depths. Similarly, you can identify with both the outer world and the inner world. While looking at the outer life, you see dynamism and speed. But even while you are looking at the outer life you can dive into the inner life, where it is all peace and inner poise. If you dive within and become inseparably one with inner peace, then easily you can bring inner peace to the fore so that it inundates your outer life.

In the morning
Meditate on the waves and surges
Of the ocean.
You will find dynamic life-energy.

In the evening
Meditate on the deep vastness
Of the ocean.
You will feel Infinity's peace.

189

Healing an injury

Healing an injury is a matter of inner capacity. One kind of capacity is to heal the injury by bringing down peace and light from Above. Another kind of capacity is to ignore the pain altogether. During your meditation, if all of a sudden you have intense aspiration, then you can bring down more light from above to cure your injury. But you have to do this consciously during your meditation. If during the day you casually say, "Oh, how I wish I didn't have any pain!" that will be useless. But while you are meditating, if you suddenly remember your pain, that is the time to pray and bring down more light.

Everything has to depend on prayer and meditation. Again, outer therapy is also of supreme need. Of course, the most important thing is the inner prayer. But it is like a boxer using two hands. With one hand you cannot do everything. You should take as much help from medical science as possible, and at the same time you have to think of our spiritual science, which is prayer and meditation. They have to go side by side.

Again, you can increase your capacity to tolerate pain. If the pain is bearable, try to run according to your own capacity. At that time, do not think of how fast this person or that person is running. Just go according to your own capacity and remain cheerful.

Offer the results to God

There are three ways you can look at sports. One way is to defeat others and show how great you are; this is the human way or animal way. This way says, "By hook or by crook I will defeat somebody and I will be the first." The second way, the divine way, is to make progress, for God Himself is progressing in and through us. This way says, "I will do my best, I will try to excel. If I did a five metre long jump, I will try to do a five and a half metre long jump and make progress." The third way, the supreme way, is to leave it entirely in the hands of the Supreme, the Eternal Pilot: "If it is Your Will, if You want, I will have the worst possible experience of utter failure. Again, if You want, I will have the experience of the best possible victory."

You are only the witness

Before the competition starts, meditate most soulfully for five minutes. Try to make yourself feel that you are not the competitor, but that somebody else is running in and through you. You are only the witness, the spectator. Since somebody else is competing, you are at perfect liberty to watch and enjoy. While you are competing, sometimes it is very difficult to enjoy the race. Either the competitive spirit or frustration is killing you, or your body is not abiding by your mental will and you feel that you are literally dying. So many problems arise.

But before you start, if you can convince yourself that you are a divine observer and that somebody else is competing in you, through you and for you, then fear, doubt, frustration, anxiety and other negative forces will not be able to assail your mind. Once these thoughts occupy the mind, they try to enter into the vital and then into the physical. When they enter into the physical, they create tension, and this makes you lose all your power of concentration. But if you feel that you are not the competitor, if you feel that you are only observing the competition from the beginning to the end, then there will be no tension, and these forces will not attack you. This is the only way to overcome these forces and maintain the highest type of concentration from the beginning to the end.

The strength of self-transcendence
Comes from the heart's
Silver faith.

Meditations
for
everyday life

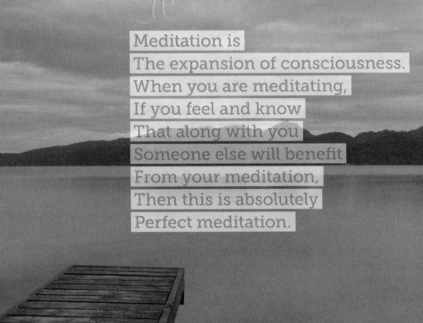

Meditation is
The expansion of consciousness.
When you are meditating,
If you feel and know
That along with you
Someone else will benefit
From your meditation,
Then this is absolutely
Perfect meditation.

Meditating on your birthday

On your birthday, early in the morning, think: "From a very, very high, higher, highest Source, I came into the world to do something really good for humanity." You have to feel at that time you are not the body, you are not the vital, you are not the mind, you are not the heart. You are only the soul.

Imagine that your soul is just entering into this world like a most beautiful little child. On your birthday, your soul is reminding Mother Earth: "I came from Above, but now I am for you. I came from God, but God has sent me only to work for you. Mother Earth, for you I have come."

Again, Mother Earth says, "You have come. You have covered such a long, long distance. Now I am giving you what I have: my concern, my affection, my blessings, my joy, my pride, my sweetness, my fondness, my tenderness—everything that I have, I am giving you and I will always give you."

Assimilating the results of meditation

There are two or three ways to assimilate into your system the light, peace or bliss you have received from a good meditation. One way is to be absolutely relaxed. This relaxation is not watching television or reading the newspaper! You should read only spiritual books.

Or you can lie down and quietly sing or hum soulful songs. If you can hum soulful songs after your deep meditation, that is the easiest and the most effective way to assimilate. You can sing yourself or listen to recordings of spiritual singing, but it will be better for you to sing. Since you have had a good meditation, you can add to your meditation with your singing. Then it will be so easy to assimilate the results of your deep, sublime meditation.

Another way is to walk very, very slowly, and let Mother Nature help you to assimilate. Very soothingly and tenderly Mother Nature will help you to assimilate all the divine things that you have received during your meditation. But Mother Nature is a great help only early in the morning or in the evening. At other times it is very difficult to get help from Mother Nature because Mother Nature has been spoiled or polluted by the restlessness of humanity. If you have a good meditation during the day, then the best thing is to sing.

Another thing you can do consciously and deliberately when you have a high experience is to breathe as slowly and quietly as possible. Try to feel that if you put a string or thread in front of your nose, it would not move.

Overcoming blocks and barriers in meditation

194

Suppose you have meditated for fifteen minutes or half an hour, and you feel frustration that you are unable to go higher. On that day give up but remember that height, and try to remember the joy of that height. Feel happy that you reached a considerable height, and keep up the ecstasy and joy.

The next day you do not have to start from the beginning and climb all the way up again. Just by using your will-power and your previous experiences, you can start very high—almost from where you stopped during your previous meditation. You know how far you went up yesterday, and from there you can try to go higher. Keep up your joy about the height you reached the previous day, and the following day make an attempt to go beyond it right from the start.

Meditating without tension

195

If you get a kind of tense feeling in your meditation, immediately breathe in very fast, and when the rhythm of your breathing increases, the tension will go away. Just imagine a flight of stairs, or a ladder that has quite a few rungs. Try to feel you are climbing up, and you are breathing in as you are climbing up. One, two, three steps: you are going up, up. If you feel this ascent, then tension goes away.

Overcoming fatigue

196

Try to invoke the Power aspect of the Supreme. Do not invoke Peace or Light; only try to bring forward divine Power from within or bring down the Power from Above. This divine Power will make you feel that your body is burning with fever, although you are not actually running a temperature, and immediately you will feel energised.

Another thing you can do is to repeat the name of the Supreme as fast as possible. It is not a race, but see how many times you can repeat 'Supreme' with each breath. Then, when you feel the power inside the repetition of this name, your whole being will be inundated with divine power and you are bound to feel a new flow of life and energy.

Always try to feel inside you a dynamic and progressive movement, but not an aggressive one. If there is a dynamic and progressive movement, then you cannot fall asleep. Inside you, feel that a train is running, running towards the destination. Feel that you yourself are an express train with only one desti-nation. The driver of that train is constantly repeating God's name to derive energy, strength, stamina and all divine qualities. An express train stops only at the end of its journey, the goal; on the way it does not stop at all. Your goal will be to reach or achieve a profound meditation.

Staying awake in meditation

Before you meditate, breathe in seven long breaths; that will help you. If you breathe very powerfully, you will energise yourself and, at the same time, conquer sleep for a few minutes.

197

You can also pinch yourself as hard as possible and try to feel that somebody else is pinching you. While you are pinching yourself, you have to know that it is your consciousness that is pinching your unconsciousness. But you have to feel that a third person is doing the pinching. Then you will say, "Stop, stop, stop!"

Overcoming lethargy

The quickest way to overcome lethargy is by repeating 'Supreme' as fast as possible. You do not have to shout at the top of your lungs, but you have to be able to hear it; do not do it in silence. You can be seated in your room or walking in a silent place where nobody is going to hear you, but you should not do it while lying down.

198

While you are chanting 'Supreme', starting with your toes imagine everything that is inside you. Think of your muscles, nerves, blood or anything that you want, and try to feel that the Supreme is entering into that particular part of your body. Then move to other parts of your body. You do not have to see what is inside your legs or your heart or your brain. Only imagine that something is there, and that that very thing is being touched by the word 'Supreme'.

If lethargy has already stationed itself inside your knee or shoulder or somewhere else, that portion of the being has to be touched by the Power of the Supreme, the Life of the Supreme and the Divinity of the Supreme. This is one of the most effective ways to conquer lethargy while walking or doing something. When you want to conquer lethargy, that is not the time for you to enter into deep meditation; only let the dynamic flow of your chanting percolate through your entire body.

Rest and sleep

There is a yogic method of getting rest. In one second you can take the rest of fifteen minutes, half an hour or even more. How can you get that kind of rest? When you go to sleep at night, feel that your whole body from head to foot has become a sea of peace. You have become peace itself. Consciously try to feel that you are not the body, but an infinite expanse of peace. When you can consciously feel this peace, you will see that your physical body has merged with it and totally disappeared in the sea of peace. If you can do this exercise effectively, you will need very little sleep.

Meditation brings down peace. This peace energises the entire body. When your whole body is surcharged with peace, you do not need so many

199

hours of rest. Sometimes two hours of rest will give you ample energy.

Early in the morning when you find it difficult to get up, try to feel that your entire body, from head to foot, represents a sea of peace. Feel that you have become peace itself that you embody peace within and without. Peace can act like dynamic strength. You feel that when the body is active and moving to and fro, you have strength; but real strength exists in inner peace, not in outer action. When you possess peace in infinite measure, you possess the source of ordinary dynamic energy. If you call upon dynamic energy, which is inside you in the form of peace, then you can get up easily.

Also, when you go to bed, just try to feel that you are going to sleep for twenty-four hours. Then, even though the clock will say that you have slept only three or four hours, your very first thought as soon as you wake up should be that you have slept for twenty-four hours. The mind can convince the outer consciousness, and immediately you will believe it. This is not self-deception; it is proper use of the conscious mind. The figure twenty-four has enormous strength. It immediately gives us a sense of comfort, relief, pleasure, fulfilment.

Meditating for spiritual dreams

200

If you want to have dreams from the higher worlds and not from the lower worlds, then before you go to sleep meditate for at least five minutes on your navel centre and the centres below the navel. This you will do in order to lock the doors to these centres. Then meditate for another five minutes on your heart centre and on the centres above the heart. This you will do in order to unlock the doors to these centres.

While locking the navel centre and the lower centres, try to feel the dynamic and volcanic energy of the hero-warrior. While unlocking the heart centre and the higher centres, try to feel the cheerfulness and delight of a child. If you can do this, without fail you are bound to have dreams from the higher worlds.

Dreams from the higher worlds

201

If you want to have dreams from the higher worlds and not from the lower worlds, then before you go to sleep, meditate for at least five minutes on your navel centre and the centres below the navel. This you will do in order to lock the doors to these centres. Then meditate for another five minutes on your heart centre and on the centres above the heart. This you will do in order to unlock the doors to these centres.

While locking the navel centre and the lower centres, try to feel the dynamic and volcanic energy of the hero-warrior. While unlocking the heart centre and the higher centres, try to feel the cheerfulness and delight of a child. If you can do this, without fail you are bound to have dreams from the higher worlds.

Chanting for physical strength

If you are physically weak, if your physical constitution is not satisfactory, you can chant sincerely and soulfully:

Tejohasi tejomayi dhehi
Viryamasi viryam mayi dhehi
*Valam masi valam mayi dhehi**

In a week's time you will see a change for the better in your health. This chant means:

I pray for dynamic energy;
I pray for dynamic virility;
I pray for indomitable physical strength.

(* for sanskrit pronunciation see the end notes)

Overcoming pain

203

You should try to invoke light in order to cure pain. Pain is, after all, a kind of darkness within us. When the inner light or the light from Above starts functioning in the pain itself, then the pain is removed or transformed into joy. Advanced seekers can actually feel joy in the pain itself. But for that, one has to be very highly advanced. In your case, during your prayer or meditation you should try to bring down light from Above and feel that the pain is a darkness within you. If you bring down light, then the pain will either be illumined and transformed or removed from your system.

Losing weight

204

You can meditate every day to lose weight. As soon as you start meditating, you have to think of yourself as a feather. You can keep a feather in front of you and feel that you are that feather. If your concentrative will-power is focussed on that feather, and if you can become one with the feather-consciousness, no matter what you eat, you will be able to lose weight. Your goal is not to become as light as a feather—far from it! The feather is only symbolic of lightness. If you can keep inside your mind a fixed idea that you are light, automatically the mind will put pressure on the physical. Imagination is a very strong power. Your imagination will be able to help you.

Overcoming weaknesses

Before you go to sleep, write down on a piece
of paper all your weaknesses. Then cross them
out mercilessly. If you have jealousy, write down
'jealousy' on the piece of paper. Then write down all
your other undivine qualities. Then cross them out as
mercilessly as possible. In this way psychologically
and also intuitively you will weaken these undivine
forces. Just make your mind conscious that these are
your enemies. This is an occult operation, but anyone
can do it.

Overcoming bad habits

Before you do anything, always meditate for a minute
or at least for a few seconds. The power of that meditation will enter into your bad habits like an arrow.
Meditation, the soldier, will use his divine arrows
against bad habits. This is absolutely the best way.

Making correct decisions

If you want to make the correct decision, you have
to meditate most soulfully for at least ten minutes.
During this time, you must not have any thought—
good or bad. The mind has to be completely empty.
After meditating for about ten minutes, you will bring

tremendous will-power from the *third eye* and focus it on the heart. Then you will try to uncover your heart chakra. If you feel that there is something covering the heart chakra like a lid, you will just uncover it.

Once you uncover the heart chakra, you will receive a whisper. That whisper will come either in the form of light or in your own language. It will not form a sentence—only one word. The light will be connected with your vision-eye, and the connection will be there inside the heart. There we do not form sentences. But from that one syllable or one word you will be able to correctly get the message and that will be your final and infallible decision.

Absolutely do not allow your mind to tell you what to do or what not to do. You have to use only the light that is connected with your vision-eye, which you will experience inside your heart centre.

You can always do the right thing if you meditate and meditate. While you are meditating, feel that both your eyes are inside your heart, they are swimming in your heart-river. Feel that each eye is a swimmer—one is a human swimmer, and the other is a divine swimmer. These two swimmers are swimming inside your heart-river with tremendous inner joy, and this river is flowing into the sea. If you can see and feel this, then you will have inner happiness. If you have true inner happiness, you will never make a mistake.

Solving problems

Problems can be solved permanently only by identifying yourself with something very strong, very powerful, very vast. Look at the sky. How much vastness it has! Look at the ocean. How much power it has! Just throw yourself into the vastness or into the power. This is the wisest way and this way is also permanent.

Meditating for protection

When an accident or something serious is about to take place, your utterance is an expression of your inner cry. At that time you need not repeat the Name of the Supreme in a slow, prolonged manner. When danger is approaching, if you repeat 'Supreme' quickly and intensely, it is an expression of the soul's cry for immediate intervention of the divine protection.

When one is pronouncing the Supreme's Name, one has to know what the purpose is. At the time of meditation or as part of one's inner spiritual discipline, one has to say it slowly and soulfully. Even then, this does not mean that you have to prolong the word as long as possible. You can say the Name very soulfully with love, reverence and devotion at a normal speed. But in an emergency, when danger is threatening, if 'Supreme' comes from the depths of the heart like an intense cry, then it is also most soulful, although it is fast.

Meditating while driving

It is not advisable, especially for beginners, to meditate or concentrate while driving. When you become an expert in the spiritual life, you can do anything. Right now you are touching the wheel, you are touching the gas, you have to look around and be alert. A day may come when you have more capacity; at that time you can concentrate, you can meditate. But right now you can repeat the name of the Supreme slowly and quietly. Then you will not lose so much of your outer consciousness.

Sri Chinmoy has asked his students to meditate for protection for one minute before and after driving.

Meditating on our loved ones

If we feel a good thought, an illumining and fulfilling thought, then that very thought we will express and offer to our friends and dear ones. Our illumining, soulful, fulfilling thoughts will enter into our dear ones and then they, too, will have peace. So when we have inner peace, automatically it expresses itself. It spreads its qualities or capacities throughout the length and breadth of the world.

If our loved ones are not receptive to our spiritual path, if they argue with us, it is better to offer them our light silently and inwardly. At night when they are sleeping and in a peaceful consciousness, we can place all our sweetest and purest aspiration into their sleeping consciousness. By acting silently, we help them most.

Meditating for your baby or child

It is more effective and more fruitful to pray for a little baby than to meditate. When he is six or seven years old, at that time you can start to concentrate and meditate on him. But for a small child, just pray for any good qualities that you want him to have. You can observe daily how many good qualities he has and pray to God to increase them. Again, if you see certain qualities that he does not have, you can ask God to add to the good qualities that he already has.

Along with your other prayers for your sweetest child, please pray for two more things: peace and love. Pray to God to inundate the child's head with peace and to inundate his heart with love. Love he easily can understand. He loves his mother and his father so much. As soon as he sees you, he feels tremendous, boundless love.

While praying for your baby, please try to observe when he is breathing in and out. As soon as he starts to inhale, you can start your prayer; and when he releases his breath, you should finish your prayer. So you have to pray very quickly. Sometimes when you are holding him in your lap or keeping him on your shoulder or very close to you, you will be able to feel or hear him breathe, and you can match your prayer to his breathing.

But even if your imagination does not coincide exactly with the time that he is breathing in and breathing out, no harm. Your imagination has a reality of its own. In a few days you will be able to develop the capacity to synchronise your prayer with his breathing. This will be the most effective way for you to pray for whatever you want for him.

Meditating to stop criticising others

213 When you want to criticise someone, the first thing you have to do is to repeat aloud three times: "*Perhaps* he is right, *perhaps* he is right, *perhaps* he is right." Then, silently, repeat three times: "He *is* right, he *is* right, he *is* right." Then say aloud: "In this case, I might have done the same. In this case, I might have done the same. In this case, I might have done the same." Then, silently, say: "In this case, I too would have done the same. In this case, I too would have done the same. In this case, I too would have done the same."

By this time, anger will lose all its hunger for you and it will not be at all interested in devouring you. It will leave you and go elsewhere to knock at the door of somebody else.

Meditating to overcome anger

214

During your meditation, try to bring down peace, sublime and solid, from Above. Your enemy is anger. Anger's enemy is peace. Anger openly hates peace. If you invoke peace soulfully, then anger will hate you ruthlessly and never will it enter into you, your life, consciously or unconsciously.

One thing more: before you invoke peace, surrender your life-breath ten times to the Will of the Supreme. Your surrender is your safeguard. Anger: just put a "d" before anger and it becomes danger. Do not play with danger, but play constantly with your soul's surrender, your heart's surrender, your mind's surrender and your body's surrender.

Meditating for someone who is angry or upset

215

When somebody is upset, first try to invoke peace into that person's system or into yourself as quickly as possible. It may be extremely difficult to bring peace into him at that moment because that person is angry and upset. At that time he does not want to take the medicine he needs, which is peace.

But you definitely have a little peace—that is why you are able to observe that the other person is so upset. Right away invoke a very large amount of peace to descend into your entire being. You will try to become the ocean of peace. Then, like a mirror, just go and stand in front of that person. His anger will be nothing in comparison to the peace which you have invoked.

On the spiritual level, you can try to invoke peace into the system of the person who is mad and furious—which is really difficult—or to bring more peace into your own system. If the person is facing an ocean of peace, he will see that his anger is nothing in comparison to that peace.

To conquer nervousness

216

When you are nervous, immediately say, "My name is confidence, my life's name is confidence. I am not only my confidence, but also God's all-knowing Confidence."

Then take a deep breath and say: "O my heart, I am with you. Do not be nervous. O my mind, I am with you. Do not be nervous. O my vital, I am with you. Do not be nervous. O my body, I am with you. Do not be nervous."

Then take another deep breath and say: "My body is God's all-knowing Confidence. My vital is God's all-embracing Confidence. My mind is God's all-illumining Confidence. My heart is God's all-fulfilling Confidence."

Meditating for someone who is ill

217

Before asking the Supreme to help with your prayer, first ask Him whether you are supposed to pray. Suppose somebody is very sick. You may think that if you pray for him, it will be a good thing, because he is suffering. But perhaps God wants him to have this experience at this particular time. You have to know that God is infinitely kinder than any human being could possibly be. If you pray to God, "Cure him, cure him," you may be standing in God's way. God may want to give him the experience of suffering in His own Way. So always ask God if it is His Will.

For the divine approach we need to add another dimension: "Eternal Father, if it is Your Will, please cure my dear one." You have to know if his stay on earth will really be of any help to him or to God. If he remains on earth a little longer, will he just lead an ordinary life and create more problems for himself, or will he make spiritual progress?

Meditating on someone who is dying

218

You do not have to look at the person, but put your whole concentration on his heart. First imagine a circle at his heart, and try to feel that this circle is rotating there like a disc. That means that life-energy is now revolving consciously in the aspiration or in the vessel of the person who is sick. Through your concentration and meditation, you are entering into the heartbeat of that person.

When you enter into the heartbeat, then your consciousness and the aspiring or dying consciousness of the other person rotate together. While they are rotating, pray with your whole being to the Supreme, "Let Thy Victory be achieved. Let Thy Will be done through this particular individual. I want only Your Victory."

Victory does not necessarily mean that the person will be cured. No, God may have decided that this person must leave the body for a very good reason. If you pray to God in a surrendered way and if the person leaves the body, then you are fulfilling God and you are fighting for God's Victory. If God wants to take him to Heaven to do something for Him there, then naturally it is God's Victory when the person leaves the body.

If you pray for the Supreme's Victory, with your aspiration you are giving all the responsibility to the Supreme. And when you can consciously give the responsibility to the Supreme, you are doing the right thing.

Meditating on someone who has passed away

There are two ways to commune with your beloved in the inner world: with your heart's cries and with your soul's smiles. Through prayers we develop our heart's cries. Through meditations we develop our soul's smiles. One way is to cry and bind your beloved. The other way is to smile and feel that he is simply starting a new journey.

Meditating to love God more

If you start *thinking* about how to love God, you will never be able to do it. It has to be spontaneous. When you enter into a garden, you do not have to think about how you can appreciate the beautiful flowers. Immediately the vibration of the garden will come and enter into you. Immediately you will smell the fragrance and see the beauty. In the same way, we love God not by thinking, but by feeling. Feel that you have opened your heart-door. When you open up the garden gate, you do not have to run to a particular flower. Immediately you get the purity and fragrance of the flowers.

Your heart is not just a tiny muscle. It is also a garden. Once you enter your heart-garden, then definitely you will be able to see the Gardener, our Lord Supreme. You can start by imagining your heart-garden. Imagination is a world of its own. It is completely different from thinking. Thinking is constant contradiction. But when you imagine something very beautiful and soulful, it has tremendous reality, tremendous truth in it. So do not think of how to love. Just love. Love is already there inside your heart-garden.

The confidence of my life
Comes from
The love of my heart
For God.

Meditation on a spiritual Teacher

Following the Indian tradition, Sri Chinmoy's students meditate on a picture of him in his highest Transcendental Consciousness. In the following passages Sri Chinmoy is explaining how to meditate on the Transcendental photograph. Seekers following a different spiritual path can consider applying this technique to meditating on a representation of another spiritual Master such as the Saviour Christ, Lord Buddha or Sri Krishna.

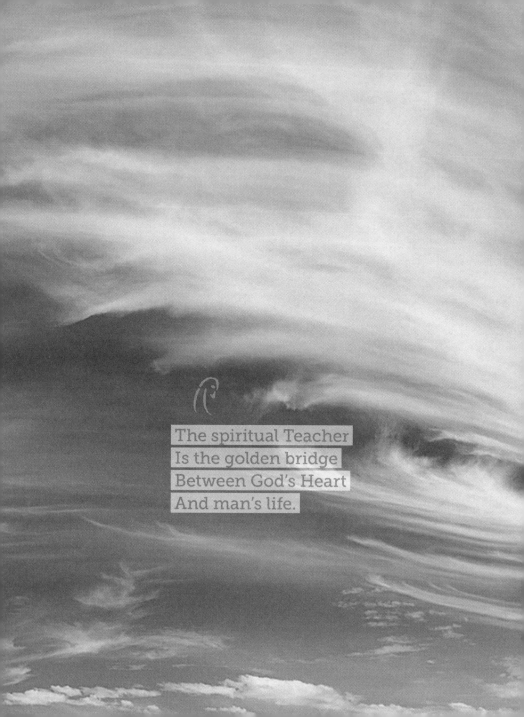

The spiritual Teacher
Is the golden bridge
Between God's Heart
And man's life.

Meditation on Sri Chinmoy's photograph

My students meditate on a picture of me taken in my transcendental consciousness. This picture embodies my highest consciousness. Again, I tell them that when they are concentrating on my picture, they are not concentrating on the physical, not on me as Sri Chinmoy, but on the Supreme in me. The Supreme is my Guru[4], your Guru, everybody's Guru.

When you want to concentrate, first look at my face, the whole face. Then gradually try to focus your attention on my forehead. Then try to think of the place in between and a little above the eyebrows—the *third eye*. Feel that only that particular spot exists and nothing else. Try to bring your eyes to that point and feel that you do not see anything else in the picture. Then try to dig there. Feel that you have a knife, a divine knife, and you dig, dig, dig. Go as deep as you can. The deeper you go, the stronger will be your power of concentration.

In your meditation,
The deeper you descend
To see your source,
The clearer becomes
Your light-road.

If you find it difficult to enter into my *third eye*, then try to breathe in slowly and steadily and imagine that I am also breathing rhythmically with you. You can be a few feet from the picture or as close as possible, but try to feel that we are breathing in and out at the same time. This will help you enter into the flow of meditation and also it will give you purity in abundant measure.

If you want to meditate, feel that the entire picture is ready to give you whatever you want. If you want peace, then look at the picture with the inner feeling that the picture has infinite peace. If you want light, if you want bliss or if you want any divine quality, just feel that the picture has it, which is absolutely true.

While meditating on my picture, you do not have to think of anything. If a thought comes, whether good or bad, just throw it into my picture. Let us say that you are jealous of someone. When you are jealous of someone, you are inwardly communicating with that person and offering him your jealous thoughts. In the same way you can throw these ideas into me. The moment you talk to me inwardly, you are giving me your thoughts.

When you concentrate on my forehead, take your time and say the word 'light' silently. While you are saying it, try to feel that you have formed a bridge between yourself and me. In a matter of a few minutes, if you have a soulful feeling of oneness with me, you are bound to see light.

Or look at my forehead in my Transcendental picture and soulfully repeat the word 'light' fifty, sixty, one hundred times. Then I assure you that you are bound to see light—either blue or white or gold or red or green—because from my transcendental consciousness I am ready to offer light to anybody who sincerely wants it. This is the secret that I am telling you.

God is the only Teacher

When you meditate on my picture and enter into my consciousness, you should not feel that you are entering into a foreign element or a foreign person, but that you are entering into your own highest part, your true self. You have a mother and a father, you have a husband or wife, you have children; now you can add one more person to your family. You have to feel that here is someone who is your own—not only for this life, but forever. If you feel your oneness with me, if you feel that I am not a foreigner but a member of your own family, then automatically your consciousness, your soul, will try to associate with mine. This very association will be meditation for you.

If you look at a tree, you become one with the consciousness of the tree. If you look at a flower, you become one with the fragrance of the flower.

Similarly, if you look at a picture of me in a very high consciousness, you become one with my inner divinity and reality. Sometimes when you see the ocean of light inside me, you may feel that if you enter into the ocean you will be drowned, overpowered, destroyed. At that time light is trying to enter into you and you are trying to hide. But you have to know that divine light will not expose you; it only wants to illumine you. The more light you receive, the sooner you will be illumined.

But if you feel fear, then it is better for you not to try to enter into me. Instead, you should allow me to enter into you. You can say, "Let the ocean of light come into me in a very, very small quantity, or let just a few drops of light enter into me." Your inner progress depends on your strength and receptivity, on how much of my spiritual food you can eat. If you have great inner strength, if you feel that you are strong enough to swim in the sea of light and bliss, then enter into me. Otherwise, let me enter into you. But this is only for seekers who want to follow my path.

Those who are not my disciples may think that it is the height of folly for anyone to meditate on my picture. Perhaps they feel that I am shamelessly proud. But I can assure you, a picture taken of me when I am in a very high consciousness, when I am totally one with the Supreme, does not represent my physical body or human personality. It does not represent Chinmoy Kumar Ghose. When my disciples meditate in front of my picture, they feel that they are meditating not in front of me but in front of their real Guru, who is the Supreme. The Supreme is the eternal Guru—my Guru, your Guru, everybody's Guru. But I represent Him in a personal, accessible way for those who have faith in me, just as there are other Masters who represent the Supreme for their disciples.

So when you meditate on my picture, please do not think of it as a picture of a human being. Think of the achievement and the consciousness that the picture represents. For my disciples, at least, my picture represents someone who has attained oneness with the Highest. If anyone concentrates on my picture with real devotion and aspiration, I have to help him.

Photograph by Ranjana

About the author

Sri Chinmoy was born in the village of Shakpura in East Bengal, India (now Bangladesh) in 1931. He was the youngest of seven children in a devout family. In 1944, after the passing of both of his parents, he joined his brothers and sisters at the Sri Aurobindo Ashram, a spiritual community near Pondicherry in South India. He meditated for several hours a day, having many deep inner experiences. It was here that he first began writing poetry to convey his widening mystical vision. He also took an active part in Ashram life and was a champion athlete for many years.

Heeding an inner command, Sri Chinmoy moved to the United States in 1964 to be of service to spiritual aspirants in the Western world. During the 43 years that he lived in the West he opened more than 100 meditation Centres worldwide and served as spiritual guide to thousands of students. Sri Chinmoy's boundless creativity found expression not only in poetry and other forms of literature, but also in musical composition and performance, art and sport. In each sphere he sought to convey the diverse experiences that comprise the spiritual journey: the search for truth and beauty, the struggle to transcend limitations, and the supremely fulfilling communion of the human soul with the Divine.

As a self-described student of peace who combined Eastern spirituality and Western dynamism in a remarkable way, Sri Chinmoy garnered international renown. In 1970 at the request of U Thant, the third Secretary-General of the United Nations, he began the twice-weekly peace meditations for delegates and staff members at UN headquarters that continued until the end of his life. Sri Chinmoy enjoyed a special friendship with many international luminaries including President Mikhail Gorbachev, Mother Teresa, President Nelson Mandela and Archbishop Desmond Tutu.

On 11 October 2007, Sri Chinmoy passed behind the curtain of Eternity. His creative, peace-loving and humanitarian endeavours are carried on worldwide by his students, who practise meditation and strive to serve the world in accordance with his timeless teachings.

For more information about Sri Chinmoy kindly visit:

www.srichinmoy.org

Learn to meditate with the Sri Chinmoy Centre

Sri Chinmoy Centres give meditation classes in over 350 cities all over the world. Sri Chinmoy asked his students to offer these classes to the general public free of charge, as he felt that the inner peace that meditation could bring was the birthright of each individual.

Find a meditation class near you at
www.srichinmoycentre.org

Recommended books of Sri Chinmoy

Meditation: Man-Perfection in God-Satisfaction

Meditation offers a structured and systematic introduction to meditation, progressing on to more advanced practices including mantras and creative visualizations and offering many practical guidelines for those seeking peace of mind in our modern world.

Sport & Meditation: The Inner Dimension of Sport

In this remarkable book, Sri Chinmoy reveals the inner aspect of sport, and world champions such as Carl Lewis, Tegla Loroupe, Paul Tergat and Bill Pearl share their own inner secrets and spiritual perspective on training and competition.

www.sportandmeditation.com

Heart-Wisdom-Drops: Inspiring Aphorisms for Every Day

This collection of 55 inspirational cards makes an excellent gift. Each card features an aphorism and meditative painting by Sri Chinmoy. For those seeking hope, peace of mind and life-wisdom these cards offer inspiration, and are a guide to a happy, harmonious and spiritually-grounded daily life.

www.wisdom-cards.com

For more books kindly visit

www.srichinmoybooks.com

Explanatory notes

1. ***The Spiritual Heart*** / The spiritual heart is located right in the centre of the chest. If you find it difficult to meditate on the spiritual heart, you can concentrate on the physical heart in the chest. But after you meditate there for a few months or for a year, you will feel that inside the ordinary human heart is the divine heart, and inside the divine heart is the soul. When you feel this, you will start meditating on the spiritual heart.

2. ***Supreme*** / There is one God called by many different names. I like the term 'Supreme'. All religious faiths have the same God but they address Him differently. A man will be called 'Father' by one person, 'Brother' by another and 'Uncle' by another. Similarly, God is also addressed in various ways, according to one's sweetest, most affectionate feeling. Instead of using the word 'God', I use the word 'Supreme' most of the time. When we say 'Supreme', we are speaking of the Supreme Lord who not only reaches the absolute Highest, but all the time goes beyond, beyond and, transcends the Beyond.

3. ***The Third Eye*** / Third Eye, also called Ajna chakra, is located between and a little above the eyebrows. It is the most powerful centre. He who has mastery over the Ajna chakra destroys his dark past, hastens the golden future and manifests the present in a supremely fulfilling way.

4. **Guru** / Guru is a Sanskrit word which means 'he who illumines'. The one who offers illumination is called

a Guru. According to my own inner realisation I wish
to say that there is only one real Guru, and that is
the Supreme. No human being is the real Guru. But
although the Supreme alone is the real Guru, here on
earth we value time. If we find someone who can help
us on our journey towards illumination, we take his
help, and we may call him our Guru.

5. **Chakras** / There are three principal channels through
   which this life-energy flows. These channels meet
   together at six different places. Each meeting place
   forms a centre. Each centre is round like a wheel.
   Indian spiritual philosophy calls these centres chakras.
   All real spiritual Masters, from the very depth of their
   experience, say that it is better to open the heart centre
   first and then try to open the other centres.

6. **AUM** / Aum is a syllable with a special significance
   and creative power. Aum is the mother of all mantras.
   When we chant AUM, what actually happens is that
   we bring down Peace and Light from above and create
   a universal harmony within and without us. When
   we repeat AUM, both our inner and our outer beings
   become inspired and surcharged with divine Light and
   aspiration. AUM has no equal. AUM has infinite Power.
   Just by repeating AUM, we can realise God.

7. **The Crown Centre** / There are seven major psychic
   centres in our body. These centres are not in the
   physical, but in the subtle body. At the crown of the
   head is one called Sahasrara, the thousand-petalled
   lotus. Sahasrara is the highest, the most peaceful, the

most soulful, the most fruitful of all the centres. When one enters into this crown centre, he enters into trance and goes beyond the consciousness of this world.

8. **Japa** / Japa is the repetition of a mantra. AUM is a mantra; it is not japa. If you repeat AUM twice, thrice or hundreds of times, this repetition is japa. A mantra can be one syllable, many syllables or even a few sentences. When we repeat the mantra, it becomes japa. Japa should be done in the morning or during the day. Japa should not be done just before going to bed.

9. **The Vital** / Each human being is composed of five elements: body, vital, mind, heart and soul. There are two vitals in us: one is the dynamic vital and the other is the aggressive vital. The vital embodies either divine dynamism or hostile aggression. When the aspirant brings the soul's light to the fore, the hostile aggression changes into the divine dynamism and the divine dynamism is transformed into the all-fulfilling supreme Reality. Emotion and the vital are two different things. You can say that the vital is the house and in that house emotion is the tenant. The most predominant emotion is the vital emotion. But emotion can also be in the body, in the mind and in the heart.

10. **The Bhagavad Gita** / The Gita is an episode in the sixth book of the Mahabharata. "Mahabharata" means "Great India," India the Sublime. This unparalleled epic is six times the size of the Iliad and the Odyssey combined. The main story revolves around a giant rivalry between two parties of cousins. Their ancestral

kingdom was the apple of discord. This rivalry came to its close at the end of a great battle called the Battle of Kurukshetra.

There are eighteen chapters in the Gita. Each chapter reveals a specific teaching of a particular form of Yoga. The Gita is the Song Celestial, sung by Lord Krishna himself. The Gita is the essence of all Indian scriptures.

11. **The Navel Centre** / The navel chakra or Manipura, the third chakra. This chakra should not be opened up until the heart centre is opened up. If the navel centre is opened before the heart, then the lowest vital, the most impure vital, may enter into the heart and destroy all your spiritual possibilities. The navel centre is also the emotional centre (see also *The Vital*).

These explanatory notes were selected from Sri Chinmoy's writings.

Sources

Meditation exercises in this book have been selected and slightly edited/shortened from the following original texts by Sri Chinmoy. Many of them are available in the English original at www.SriChinmoyLibrary.com.

A Galaxy of Beauty's Stars
A Life of Blossoming Love
Creation and Perfection
Death and Reincarnation
Earth's Cry Meets Heaven's Smile, *Part 3*
Earth's Dream-Boat Sails
Ego and Self-Complacency
Eternity's Journey
Eternity's Soul-Bird, *Part 1*
Flame-Waves, *Parts 10 a 12*
God the Supreme Musician
God-Journey's Perfection Return
Hunger of Darkness and the Feast of Light, The, *1 & 2*
Inner Peace and World Peace
Inner Running and the Outer Running, The
Inner World and Outer World, The
Kundalini: The Mother Power
Meditation: God Speaks and I Listen, *Part 1*
Meditation: God's Blessing-Assurance
Meditation: God's Voice and Man's Choice, *Part 1*
Meditation: Humanity's Race and Divinity's Grace, *Part 1*
Meditation: Man-Perfection in God-Satisfaction
Meditation-World, The

Mind-Confusion and Heart-Illumination
My Heart-Melody
Oneness-Reality and Perfection-Divinity
Perfection in the Head-World
Prayer-World, Mantra-World and Japa-World
Problems! Problems! Are They Really Problems?
Purity-River Wins
Simplicity, Sincerity, Purity and Divinity
Sound and Silence, *Part 1*
Sri Chinmoy Answers, *multiple parts*
Sri Chinmoy Speaks, *Part 5*
Ten Thousand Flower-Flames, *multiple parts*
Two Divine Instruments: Master and Student
Twenty-Seven Thousand Aspiration-Plants, *multiple parts*
United Nations Meditation-Flowers and To-Morrow's Noon
You are Your Life Progress-Joy-Drum

Some exercises have been taken from various editions of magazines which are no longer available:

Aum
Chinmoy Family
Jharna-Kala

Notes

....

....

....

....

....

....

....

....

....

....

....

....

....

....

....